Symphonies of the Wild-Hearted

—An Anthology of Poems—

Austie M. Baird
—Editor & Cover Artist—

Austie M. Baird is a born and raised Oregonian, holding both History and Education degrees from Eastern Oregon University. Long before becoming a wife and mother, Baird connected with the power of the written word, finding healing properties in both reading and writing. She draws strength from the beauty that surrounds her and the overwhelming love of her family.

A.B.Baird Publishing
Oregon, USA

Copyright © 2019 by A.B.Baird Publishing
All rights reserved. This book or any portion thereof may not be reproduced or used in any manner whatsoever without the express written permission of the publisher except for the use of brief quotations in a book review.

Printed in the United States of America

First Printing, 2019

ISBN: 978-1-949321-08-1
Library of Congress Number: 2019952520
All writings within this anthology belong to the author to which they are credited. Contributing authors maintain the copyrights for each piece submitted and published within this anthology.

Cover Art Image by Austie M. Baird

A.B.Baird Publishing
66548 Highway 203
La Grande OR, 97850
USA

www.abbairdpublishing.com

−Table of Contents−

Dedications	p. 5-6
Sara Kelly	
Biography	p. 7
Poems	p. 8-19
Otthilia Poetria	
Biography	p. 20
Poems	p. 21 – 38
Barry Hollow	
Biography	p. 39
Poems	p. 40 - 63
L. T. Pelle	
Biography	p. 64
Poems	p. 65 - 78
Adeline Gray	
Biography	p. 79
Poems	p. 80 - 106
Alan J.	
Biography	p. 107
Poems	p. 108 – 142
Emily May Portillo	
Biography	p. 143
Poems	p. 144 – 170
Emma Blas	
Biography	p. 171
Poems	p. 172 – 199
Lucia Haase	
Biography	p. 200
Poems	p. 201 - 213

−Table of Contents Continued−

Jessica Walsh
    Biography   p. 214
    Poems   p. 215 − 234
Wildflower
    Biography   p. 235
    Poems   p. 236 − 252
Author Information   p. 253

— Dedications —

To my nephews & nieces: Ethan, Kaylee, Jovan, Jayce, & Sarah
 — *Ann J.*

Dedication to Jesus and my family.
 — *Lucia Haase*

To Chima, Azalee and my parents for their, love, support and inexhaustible ability to put up with my ramblings.
 — *Barry Hollow*

To my ever supportive family, and my loving husband.
 — *Sara Kelly*

I wish to dedicate these poems to the verdant landscape of Asturias, to Spain, to Mother Earth for her never-ending inspiration and support and to you reading, for without you poems are just words on paper.
 — *Emma Blas*

For those who believed in me. Thank you. And for Darian and Ronan. You'll never know how much I love you. But, it's more. I love you the most, times infinity. I win.
 — *Emily May Portillo*

To J, my great love, thank you for believing in me
 — *Adeline Gray*

Symphonies of the Wild-Hearted

For Claire, Kate, Woogie, Jen and all my other wild women. I admire your strength. I admire your hearts.
— L. T. Pelle

To my parents—for always allowing me to dream, catch fireflies, explore the woods, and get my feet dirty.
— Wildflower

To everyone who believes in me. Thank you.
— Otthilia Poetria

For Olivia and Michael, the pieces that complete the beautiful puzzle of my life
— Jessica Walsh

Sara Kelly

@sara_kelly_poetry

Sara Kelly is 26 years old, and resides in Northeast Ohio. She has earned degrees in Heath Services Administration, as well as Physical Therapist Assisting, and although she works full time within the field of healthcare by day, she is a poet at heart. Sara derives most of her inspiration from her love of nature, as well as her profession. She has previously had work published in the anthologies entitled *Wildflower Warriors*, Her Heart Poetry's *The Annual*, and *Gratitudes: To Our Mothers*. She was also a contributing author in the first edition of Nightingale and Sparrow's online literary magazine, entitled Flight.

—Breathe—
Branches of the great oak,
blooming alveoli,
of a world turned green.

The conductor of intricate artistry,
creator of air.
Can I bring this page back to life?
Could I possibly make
these words breathe?

— Sara Kelly

—Brokenness—
Millions of years past,
Pangea mothers seven
through the breaking of one,
and they are borne home
on the back of a vast ocean

*There is certainly
beauty in this breaking.*

— Sara Kelly

—Violet—

Letters from the sun
are received by the
soft glow of an
early morning moon.
A violet good night
brushes gently against
the quiet light of dawn.

We are the background noise
in the love story between
the actuality of today,
and the hope of tomorrow.

- Sara Kelly

—Aftertaste—

Wet Earth beneath
eager feet is the aftertaste
of a cold winter,
and the product of
fresh spring rain.

It is the canvas
of the masterpiece
that is wildflowers
and perennials,
and the major contributor to
all the new beginnings.

- Sara Kelly

Symphonies of the Wild-Hearted

—Petals—

You are going to have days
when you feel lower
than the dirt beneath
your pretty feet.

Just remember,
the loveliest flowers
require not only sunshine,
but rich soil,
if they are to display
the beauty of their petals.

— Sara Kelly

—Blustery—

Blow worries away
with blustery winds, and may
good thoughts find shelter.

— Sara Kelly

—Veins—

The Ohio gushes
through a green valley.
A sky without a cloud
makes muddy waters
look ever so clear.

Post thaw,
the pulse of Mother Earth,
it beats strong.
The ice in her veins will melt
as the temperature starts to climb.

Blood flows freely,
and all the things
that are wild
know that it is finally
a safe space to grow.

— Sara Kelly

—Mending—

Broken shards are mended
under a blanket of stars.
Plant the remains of the repaired,
so that this morning glory heart
may bloom at the first sign
of the rising sun.

— Sara Kelly

Symphonies of the Wild-Hearted

—Continuing—

The creek flows until it meets the river.
The river continues to progress
along its chosen path,
and the estuary,
it is the finish line.
Once it is crossed,
the river is spilled out
into the victory of the ocean.

No matter how small you may feel,
it is important to always
keep moving forward.

— Sara Kelly

—Rise—

As the sun rises,
it says goodbye to the moon
by painting the sky
with its gorgeous hues.
Consequently, the moon yearns
to kiss the dawn in gratitude,
but instead, it allows the brilliance
of the pigmentation
to awaken the world.

— Sara Kelly

—Residue—
If I choose to caress
the night sky,
will even the gentlest touch
create ripples in the anterior surface
of this atmosphere we behold?

Will others notice
this disturbance,
and take note of
the residue
the universe will surely
leave on my hands?

- Sara Kelly

—Tides—
Hundreds of miles inland she stands,
and yet, it beckons her.
Although its energy is married to the moon,
the seduction is magnetic.
It engulfs her.

- Sara Kelly

—Storms—

She was the quiet type,
but had always related more to the
most severe of thunderstorms
than she did to other members
of the human race.

The silent accumulation of energy
in the surrounding atmosphere
was much more appealing to her
than dull conversations about the weather.

— Sara Kelly

—Ghost—

Spirit is in eyes
as gold as the fallen leaves.
The ghost of a smile
played upon lips
red as the rose,
the rose long gone.
Gone is the rose
with the waning warmth,
but the thorns, they remain.
Although they remain still,
the vessel will not possess
this barbed wire heart,
for the soul is freed
with the cool Autumn breeze.

— Sara Kelly

—Fairest—
We are not always
The fairness of the rose,
But we are often the thistle,
We are often the thorn.

*And that will always
be quite alright.*

- Sara Kelly

—Grass Stains—
Blades without the
danger of puncture.
Green stains are the only
mark that is left on the
underside of toes, shoeless.
Bring forth the buttercup,
place it beneath lips of laughter,
under the chin upon which
the smile sits.
The subtlety of sourgrass
lingers on a tongue
that rests within a body
embraced by the sun's rays.

- Sara Kelly

Symphonies of the Wild-Hearted

—Relatable—

I am in love
with the way
the pale underbelly
of every leaf
contrasts to the deep
indigo of a threatening sky.

I am more akin
to these fierce winds
than I am to
flesh and bone.

— Sara Kelly

—Spreading—

If I plunge these hands
into the soil,
will these words
I hold in my heart
travel through my fingertips
to create a more
fertile ground?

Will a piece of me
be left behind
to grow along with all
of these other things
I intend to cultivate?

Will it cover these grounds,
and invade the hearts of others
with English ivy fingers,
a green mirror to a blue sky?

*Go ahead and take a
peek at the reflection.
I want you to see how lovely
it all really is.*

— Sara Kelly

—Gratitude—
If only I could profess
the eternal adoration
that I harbor for each
and every tiny drop
that plummets to the Earth.

Clinging to hair,
and racing down a rosy cheek,
if only I could express my gratitude.
For without this nourishment,
how in the world
would all the wild things grow?

- Sara Kelly

—Some days—
There are days when
I am the wind.
Hear me whisper,
feel me brush gently
against bare arms.

I am here,
and then I am gone.

- Sara Kelly

Symphonies of the Wild-Hearted

—Clear skies—
I will drown the boredom
of this everyday life in
the brilliant blue
of a clear sky.

Let me take a long draught
of sunshine. It will quench
the thirst that I have acquired
for the warmth that we all
crave far too often.

— Sara Kelly

—Grounded—
Even after all this time,
I wouldn't want to be
anywhere else.

Here, we stand upon
layers of rich clay.

Our roots run deep.

— Sara Kelly

—North wind—
Frigid gales sculpt snow fields
while Jack Frost converses
with the man in the cold moon.
Within a sparkling landscape,
the masterpiece is born
from the breath of the North Wind.

Conversation ends,
and all pause and stare,
for the icy breeze,
and the beauty of the scene
abducts the breath
of the artist,
and the spectators.

- Sara Kelly

Otthilia Poetria

@otthilia__poetria

Otthilia is a Dutch poetess. In April 2017 she started sharing her poetry on Instagram. She writes about topics such as love, lust, heartbreak, mental illness, and surviving emotional abuse. She was featured on Untwine.Me's '100 Inspiring Instagrammers of 2017', 'Top 50 Instapoets of April 2018' and '100 Incredible Instapoets of 2018'. She was also featured on A Voice from Far Away's 'Top 10 Emerging Female Poets of Instagram' in April 2018.

—Lost—

As rivers drown
And willows weep,
I wander through the days.
The flowers won't grow anymore
And the roads have all gone grey.
My heart used to stand tall,
But mountains started to crumble,
As my mind began to break.
It's all clouds now,
Overcast and haunting,
Down there in the valley
Where my entangled roots reside.
And as willows weep
And rivers drown,
I have lost my way.

- Otthilia Postria

−Cold−

Smiling like a river
I float
Your eyes like porcelain
Stories told by stones
Hands outstretched
Reaching
Cold
Take me in
Take me home.

- Otthilia Poetria

−The woods of my sorrow−

I'm lost in the woods of my sorrow.
I can't seem to retrace the path
That leads back into the open.
It's so dark here.
It's so damn dark.

- Otthilia Poetria

—A memory of rain—
Oh how I fell,
When the clouds no longer held me
In their embrace.
Everything became a blur.
The earth welcomed my broken bones
And healed them in the soil.
But I lay there with broken spirit,
Reaching for branches that only I could see.
Looking at the sky
And hoping that it would take on
The colour of forgiveness.
As all I was now was petrichor,
A memory of rain.

— *Otthilia Poetria*

Symphonies of the Wild-Hearted

— I was a summer once —

I was a summer once.
A golden-haired sun,
Sultry heat from long days and short nights
Emitting from my skin.
I was meadows filled with flowers
And butterflies dancing in the wind.
He came looking for my honey once,
The boy with the riverbed eyes.
He circled me like a bee
And when we collided
A sea of petals opened,
The sky was painted in hues
Of orange, pink and gold,
And the world was turned into
A kaleidoscope of colours.
But nothing lasts forever
And the heat of summertide
Had to make way for rain.
The riverbed that had gone dry,
Now was filled again with water.
Rivers have to run their course,
So my boy left me
And I turned into autumn.

— Otthilia Poetoria

—How many more seasons—
The spring flowers have wilted,
The bulbs have gone back to sleep.
The lilac season came and went
And took its fragrant flowers with it.
Now summer has arrived
And the air is heavy
With the scent of linden trees.
The lavender is growing
And the roses have started to bloom.
Soon I'll be buying sweet peas
For the little vases in my room.
Summer has arrived,
But you still haven't.
How many more seasons
Must come and go,
Before you will appear?

- Otthilia Poetria

—Hands like oceans—
Fingers pulling away
Like the tide.
Only to return when
You are looking for a shore.
Hands like oceans.

- Otthilia Poetria

Symphonies of the Wild-Hearted

—Watercolour girl—
The jackdaws had always been my friends,
Telling me stories the wind had carried to them.
I took all the pebbles I could find,
To build the castles in my mind;
My strongholds for when it all became too much.
I would be staring at the tree branches,
Whenever I was looking for an embrace.
The fog of sadness twirling around me.
You could find me whispering to cats,
As we tend to understand each other;
Smiling with our eyes.
I was a watercolour girl:
Colourful, yet always mixed with rain.

— Otthilia Poetria

—Wash me clean—
My words collided with the clouds
And turned into a wave of birds.
Sorrow wrapped in wings,
Wash over me.
Baptize me with your feathers,
Wash me clean.

— Otthilia Poetria

—Narcissist—
I was like a blossom tree.
You shook all my branches vehemently
To make me lose my flowers.
You didn't like to see me happy.
You didn't like to see me do well.
So my spirit had to be broken.
My flowers had to fall.

- Otthilia Poetria

—Waiting—
And when you leave,
You take my whole world with you.
And I am here, *waiting*.
Waiting for the seasons to change
And for the winds to bring you back.

- Otthilia Poetria

Symphonies of the Wild-Hearted

—Valleys of destruction—

Valleys of destruction
Are the lines that run
Across the palms of your hands;
Just as menacing as the lines
That roll off your tongue.
You broke rivers,
You broke streams;
Stepping stones all gone.
You burned the night sky red
And left the ashes of incinerated stars
At the feet of the beloved,
Making her eyes swim in despair.
Plunging her into the vast blackness
Of the nocturnal tide,
Won't make you the master of your demons.
The euphoria of triumph will soon fade away,
When you realize you live
Under the same vault of heaven.
You burned to ashes and dust
The guiding lights of the celestial ceiling
And now the darkness is closing in.

— *Otthilia Poetria*

―The autumn of your love―

The atmosphere is humming,
I can feel it in my bones;
It's the autumn of your love for me.
Words are falling like leaves,
And every leaf that hits the ground
Causes a vibration
That cracks the earth we stand on.
The cracks turn into trenches,
Trenches into an abyss.
The humming intensifies,
Until there are no more leaves left
To drop from our branches
And there appears a sweeping silence,
The type of silence only winter can bring.

- Otthilia Poetria

—Smoke and shadows—

I walk with shadows
Down the roads less travelled, off the beaten path.
Always taking the sunset with me wherever I go.
I remind lonely souls of that burning, dying light.
Of blood oranges and cinnamon.
Followed by night air scented with sandalwood and jasmine,
As my voice brings in the dusk.

Speak to me, they say.
Speak to me of smoke and shadows.

That is how they want to hear me,
That is how they want to hold me.

Smoke and shadows,

Good for the candle-lit hours.

Enchanted by the flickering of flames.

Smoke and shadows,

There to ease their anxiety and pain
With soft-spoken syllables and touch of skin.

Smoke and shadows,

Good for the lonely night hours,
But no longer wanted after dawn.

— Otthilia Poetria

—Your garden—

Don't plant seeds of hope in my heart,
Just to keep me in your garden.
*I don't deserve to be just another option
In a row of pretty flowers.*

— Otthilia Postria

—The last petal of hope—

Between the flowers
Is where you can find me sleeping;
Clinging to the last petal of hope.

— Otthilia Postria

—Souls of one galaxy—

I'm bleeding night skies
And every star carries your name.
I'm leaking love into constellations.
*We are the souls of one galaxy,
Yet I never seem to reach you.*

— Otthilia Postria

Symphonies of the Wild-Hearted

—Sea of bitterness—

They should have named you Mary.
You with your sea-coloured eyes,
So bitter and so beautiful.
How long have you been standing on that cliff,
Staring into the endless blue?
He can't hear or see you now,
His ship is too far away.
But Lady of Sorrow, you're not alone.
Feel how the Zephyr picks you up
And cradles you in its diaphanous arms.
Its wind will carry your tears
And spread them
Like dew drops of the morning,
Coating every blade of grass with the message:
Forget me not,
Forget me not,
Forget me not.

- Otthilia Poetria

—Arbor Amoris, Arbor Vitae—

I can feel the ground vibrate beneath my feet,
As I walk towards the tree;

The roots have songs.

I place my hands upon the trunk,
Feel the bark beneath my finger.
I close my eyes and think,

We could have grown a forest,
With seedlings of our own.

I climb all the way up to the crown.
I sit between the branches,
I hide beneath the leaves.
The roots have songs and I sing along,
To keep the tree alive,
While half of it is dying.

The roots have songs
And I sing along, softly.

We could have grown a forest.
We could have grown our tree.

- Otthilia Poetria

—Indelible—

I have wandered the realms of mortal minds,
Leaving footprints on the shores of their thoughts.
It takes more than a sea to wash them away,
Waves of blue and grey will not erase them.
Like a tree in a forest, I take root in your soul.
My branches reaching every corner of your conscience.
Whether I become a dream or a nightmare depends on you.
What is certain is that I will become a memory.
And you will always see my eyes
When you close yours.

- Otthilia Poetria

—Today I like the burn—

The air tastes of salt,
Impregnated with the tears shed by Hours.
It stings the bruises on my lips,
But today I like the burn.
The horizon bleeds a melody
Of murmurs long forgotten,
Blending voices with the clouds.
Grabbing threads of silver,
I unveil the grin of Time,
While mockingbirds mimic the sound
Of passing Minutes.
The air tastes of salt.
But today I like the burn.

- Otthilia Poetria

Symphonies of the Wild-Hearted

—Breath of contentment—

It was but fleeting beauty,
This breath of contentment.
The sky came to the ground
And bruised irises bloomed from sight.
The Moon with its many phases
Was just another disc thrown across the world
To silence our cries of desire
For the golden apples we still couldn't reach.
Too high. Too high.
Too close to the Sun.
Drowning caused by fire.
Wax dripping in our eyes.
Yes, it was but fleeting beauty,
This breath of contentment.

— *Otthilia Poetria*

—Conscious—

Trees of thoughts build castles in the wind
I weave a canopy of sky
To peer through the cracks of my conscious
Words float by like wisps of cloud
You are the eye of my storm
Behind fortified windows
My whole world in a drop of rain.

— *Otthilia Poetria*

—I rise—

Ascendō,

I rise.

You can try

To bury me deeper,

But a lotus flower

Grows towards the light

Through the murkiest of waters.

- Otthilia Poetria

—The one who plants a rose garden—

I weave the winds into a tapestry;

Soft summer breeze,

Combined with winter's air.

The grass grows into a lullaby;

The vines add to the rhythm,

Softly swaying in the sun.

I lie down on my bed of poppies

And reach out my hand to you.

Will you be the one

Who plants a rose garden

In my head?

- Otthilia Poetria

Symphonies of the Wild-Hearted

—Bloom—
I cannot erase your past,
But I will do everything in my power
To fill the cracks in your heart and soul
With the seeds of my love and compassion,
So that what you thought
Was an everlasting wasteland
Will be in full bloom
Once more.
Let me help you heal,
Let me help you grow.

— Otthilia Poetria

—Vespertine flower—
A vespertine flower,
I start to blossom when evening falls.
I open my petals for you,
My nocturnal lover.
For you, I will bloom
All night long.

— Otthilia Poetria

—Crashing waves & whispering leaves—
We both have multicoloured eyes,
Always changing with the light.
His are like the sea.
Mine are like a forest.
A love song
Of crashing waves
And whispering leaves.

— Otthilia Poetria

−Summer is−

Summer is...
Chasing sunsets at the beach.
Collecting seashells and memories.
Drinking English cider.
Laughing about happy accidents
And how wonderfully strange life can be.
Putting on leather jackets
And huddling together,
As temperatures drop
After the sun sinks into the sea.
Looking at the stars
In the sky and in each other's eyes.
Lighting bonfires in our hearts
With a kiss.
Summer is
Your scent on my skin
And sand in my hair.
Summer is
You and me,
Together.

— Otthilia Postria

— A nocturnal walk —

The night had a delicate beauty about it,
Like a Luna moth fluttering in pale moonlight.
My love and I were walking in the garden,
Enjoying the scents of wisteria and night-blooming jasmine
Perfuming the air around us.
The sky looked like rich, dark velvet
And my love and I gazed at the twinkling diamonds
Strewn across this nocturnal canopy.
But it wasn't long before he turned his head
To look at me in quiet adoration.
I asked him why he stopped looking at
The luminous constellations in the night sky.
He took my face in his hands and said,
"There is so much beauty around us,
But my eyes will always be drawn to you.
Because for me, your beauty is the greatest of all
And my desire to see you knows no bounds."

— Otthilia Poetria

Barry Hollow

@thehollowgram

As a child of Ayrshire in the South West of Scotland, Barry Hollow wandered a long way south to arrive in Bristol in 2003, where he has planted roots with his wonderful wife, beautiful 7 year old daughter and very Ninja-like cat, Jessie! Barry regularly writes technical documents and reports, so is enjoying the magic and creativity of making poems, where his 40 years of experiences help him reflect on life, society and the universe at large! His unique voice comes through in his poems and occasionally out of his mouth with forays into spoken word poetry. Barry recently joined North Bristol Writers Group who are a prominent body of writers within the literary community, here in the vibrant and cultured city where he lives. Barry's poetry has been published in three online literature magazines and more recently was featured in the poetry anthology, Spilled Ink. He is currently working on a manuscript for his debut poetry collection.

—Three trees—

There's a forest in my bedroom
made of multi-coloured trees
the tall one has an aura
and perennial pulsing leaves.

The one with mirrored puddles,
reflects as much as grieves
and the one that tends to life
grows hearts to wear on sleeves.

These trees were made in Scotland
by a son of River Doon
who plies polychromic vision
as he daunders roon the toon

These trunks of varied mettle
wear bark of armoured suits
one for child, wife and I;
the forest of my roots.

- Barry Hollow

—Feeding the beast—

This symbiotic demon beast,
has savage thirst and blackened taste,
devouring light with gaping maw,
as creeping doubts are easy prey,
which feeds the flames of hubris hunger.

Self-loathing of my host's disgust,
fills its lusty need for growth,
to leech upon his sickened mind,
this character of evil deeds,
cajoles him on and on to worse
with whispers of an evil curse.

But then a change it did not see,
was sudden like a fresh lit match,
and bubbling bile from which it feasts,
now arid as Mojave's plains,
and chains once cast around his heart,
are now dissolved by hope's new broth,
and disappeared with light of worth.

- *Barry Hollow*

Symphonies of the Wild-Hearted

—Humanity is in the name—

What does it mean to be human,
do you mean like a new man or woman?
Do you wake up in makeup,
having made up your mind, to be you
with your name, and a person who's kind?
Were you shook wide a-woke,
with a sense to evoke;
To sing us your song,
voices clear and un-choked?
And where is the difference,
if it's your choice or not?
this resulting equation,
equal rights to rejoice,
and speak of your name,
as a human of note!

So shut down right wingers
as they flood all our lives,
leach out acid rain,
like a stab without knives.
Yet they dish out the pain
with dark views of disdain,
then it comes in a downpour;
a deluge, a torrent.
Their bile so black it's grievous,
abhorrent, still keeps on coming,
This tsunami of blood.

Then stand up so tall,
herald humans to action,
defy selfish ways
and inhuman infraction!

Call out the guilty,
Say, please state your name,
for the sake of the record,
and these crimes, we proclaim!
Your time's at an end, with no chance
for parole, so raise a balled fist
for the strength of our soul!
With defiance and pride,
to take on the world, and no longer hide

— Barry Hollow

—Extinction—
make it personal
with blinding third eye foresight
eternal winter
of our future fossil grief
wrought tears of black extinction

- Barry Hollow

—Floating—
I give you no choice
see me,
suspended in perfect chaos
as we imprint
as i still your eternal mind's portrait
see me clear and surging
yet languid at once
surging through the murk
deep in the abyss with you
i am your vibrance
your essence

and I flood from you
yet we are singular
always entwined, never unconnected
i am your thick, crimson claret
too pure to blend
too strong to bend
to the will of this tenebrosity
we are one
and they will never unsee us

- Barry Hollow

—Whisper of a shadow—
The trailing draft of gutless fear,
Passes near the dying embers
The wildfire deep within me
Is primed, and it remembers

Volcanic heat and light
Had been so very tempered
But heed the warning now you fool
Or the reaction will not be measured

The inferno stoked will flash
With tumultuous effect
And leave naught but a whisper
Of your shadow as a wreck

- *Barry Hollow*

—It's in the bonding—

I am here to receive,
for the most private moments,
and often to send a message,
in unity of purpose.

I am the gaps in your between,
background and foreground,
giving texture and perspective,
where light and shade had no home.

I am the vessel for that which flows
from you, whether midnight malcontent,
or submarine yellow whimsy.

I have lines, invisible once,
and wrinkles of contrast,
with a wee bit of battle damage,
you could say.

Some may bring prejudices,
observing a look I had,
of vacancy, somewhat blank
and terrifying.

Though my own reflection
is of purity and confidence,
all poise and serenity,
ready for the magic of our art.

Of course, mistakes are made,
marked irregular and blotted shapes;
absorbed, bonding kinship;
harking back to the roots of us,
knots chiselled from the familiar tree;

And the time you sincerely'd
where you should have regarded me
more warmly; leaned so hard,
pushed right through thin skin
before I was torn up and tossed aside.

As we start fresh, let my lines guide you,
ensure we are on the same page,
and bound, an ink blood bond,
spines intact; keeping contact
with the bibliography before us

And I am always ready
for new adventures,
plots twists and fresh chapters,
new characters built by arrangement,
of characters you etch out with me.

- Barry Hollow

—Poseidon's whisper—

Lashed to a sea beaten post with the utmost disrespect
for the inevitable accepting tide, ready to reside in me. On kissing ankles
and prickled toes, foregoing freedom of flight as insight gained
clarity floods this vessel. I am buoyed as Poseidon's whisper is deployed
in congruence with my new view of acceptance, minus repentance for what is coming.

Then tangerine horizon sky pours out of unseeing rainbow flecked eyes,
while my true soul flies, soaring through currents,
currently pooling, currently pulling me, ripping me, rippling me in waves of
consciousness.
I drift as I would, as I might, and I deliberate how deliberately
I acquiesce, as my sea salt essence is cleansed and cleaned, more than washed up.

- *Barry Hollow*

—The last lament—

Gazing over furrows deep, while turning
clay for crops to reap, I calmed a mind too
quick of beat. And thinking back to skies
that weep, with wrath so vile its burn ran deep.
And how that scar I had to keep.
That scar was one I had to keep.

A caw was heard of winters crow, while clearing
back the drifted snow. I asked her twice of
what she'd know, of mountains, seas and
lands below; or warmth where southern rivers flow.
A tale which never told of woe.
That tale it never told of woe.

With tenfold turns of equinox, the crow and I
had many talks, of counting on our ticking
clocks. And many times I'd heed her squawks,
of lessons learned from hardy knocks.
And paths she took less orthodox
Those choices were less orthodox.

Horizons sunset slipped from sight, as feathers
spread for starry flight. Lament was sparked this howling plight,
and heart crevassed by joyless blight,
though healed at once by memories might.
And lunar sparkles cast so bright.
Those lunar sparkles cast so bright.

- Barry Hollow

—Serendipity—

Serendipity sails silently
on savage stormy seas
Prudently picks peaceful ports
and provides power to please

Lucky loquacious ladies
have learned audacious lessons
Benefiting bountifully because
of boundless blessings

Mellifluous majestic males
have mastered many miles
Worthy wondrous writings
Wrought with weathered winsome wiles

Serendipity shows serenely
She's sincerely sound and stoic
Her heaving heavy heart
is honestly, heroic.

- Barry Hollow

—Blooming—

looking mostly in this misty opaque mirror
of un-reflection
a malevolent gritty grin and grimace
of what i don't see before me
this non-reflection of non-inflection
feeling a predilection for introspection
to see if my eyes were truly open to what was inside to push outside
can I or you or they abide?
the indication and vindication
that this transformation is only indignation
at what others don't see in or out in me
without a whisper of a shadow of this doubt in me o' my
is it just pie in the blue sky thinking
that sees me drinking it all in
in the blinking that blue eyed boy
who is really Van the Man's brown eyed girl
who dreams of twirls and swirls and falling
heels over head on my bed of posies
ready to spring into the fullest summer bloom

- *Barry Hollow*

—Feeling the blues—
Feeling blue is not so bad,
for being down or slightly sad,
as I propose a different view,
of summer skies with azure hue,
or endless oceans deep and dark,
with mysteries to find and hark!
A ribbon in a daughter's hair
Or football boots she wants to wear,
colour of a rainbow strip,
or flower on a meadow trip.
The jam and cool of BB King,
moved by tones when Eta sings!
The fuzz and buzz of sparks that fly
electric zaps across the sky!
You have the right to bold opinion
to hold this tint in poor dominion,
but the way I feel and see the clues
this festival of many blues.

- *Barry Hollow*

—Horizons for connection—

head up from your chest
head up to horizons
horizons with curve
horizons to carve
carve out of mountains
carve with your mind
mind melded mood
mind peas and queues
queues round the block
queues hewn from rock
rock rolled with notes
rock someone's world
world run by fools
world hotting up
up in the ozone
up where we fly
fly in the ointment
fly in my soup
soup made of peas
soup, more sir, please
please pleases all
please just yourself
yourself as a loved one
yourself as a friend

friend of the planet
friend of earth's wealth
wealth warped insanity
wealth buys you health
health care for sale
health drained by stealth
stealth bomb destruction
stealth tears up nations
nations stood by
nations unite
unite and untie
unite all the clans
clans of one species
clans with one plan
plan to persist
plan for all time
time to resist
time of our lives
lives build reform
lives wrapped up and warm
warm by the hearth
warm by connection
connection eternal
connection through hope
hope...
eternal...

- Barry Hollow

Symphonies of the Wild-Hearted

—Making moves—

Sodden dirt
rotted rancid roots
heal happy
feet tap
dance free and clear, emboldens
heavy plant crossing

streams full
slanted slowing snow
drifting high
stakes stuck
all on black, jacked, loaded
dice for rich pickings

- Barry Hollow

—Limitless—

Languish not on unstretched laurels
Instigate vibrant intentions
Meaningfully with gusto
Inverting implosion
To reach skyward
Loading springs
Earthly wings
Soaring
Soul

- Barry Hollow

—Origins—
children of stardust
bloom with arborescence
binding humankind
with primordial cosmic glue
we reach our blissful zenith

- Barry Hollow

—Wild things—
That day
you stood
at the summit,
wore a field of buttercups
with no need to hold one
close to my face,
to see the reflect skin glow.

And as the reaching down
midday sun, sullen
no more,
eyes crinkled,
smiles and breathes,
parting the cheering clouds. Peeking
through the nimbus crowds
to shorten shadows,
as horizon haze is poured
into a brimming cup;

And the Dandy Lion dances
with maypole skips,
and admiring glances,
hand extending,
ribbon wound, round
and bound on a third finger,
causing life to bind life,
pushing roots into soil
and bonding
sticky hearts.

- Barry Hollow

Symphonies of the Wild-Hearted

—Dozy summer days—
Fuzzy feelings of buzzy beings
waking up to sky blue ceilings,
then you hear the child's laughter
and wonder who they're chasing after.

This balmy breeze floats over skin
and lover near me, leaning in,
For kisses light and kisses warm
wrapping round each other's form

Inhaling long, and breathe, in deep
contentment in my heart to keep,
these summer days that feed the soul
with quenching thirst for life's punch bowl.

A chorus of symphonic tweets
And abundant auditory treats
From feathered friends in leafy stalls
Provides the picnic score for all

Olfactory assault compiled
By garlic sweet and growing wild
My senses all, are stimulated
They're come to life and captivated

We end our day with one last ode
Across the stream by river boat
The Ferry Fairy sees us right
to sail with peace into the night

— *Barry Hollow*

— Bing sings but Walt disnae —

I drank from honeyed oceans
And I drank of cayenne sun
I drank with purple moons
Where the river used to run

The rivers gasp for air at dusk
as clouds who always wept
filled up granite beds
where the salmon never slept

The cast danced a rainbow,
Crossing bridges with urgent steps
spinning tales of fairies
where summer intersects

As sycamore hugs Jupiter
viewing murmuration throng
with tribute of the Western rush
And the new magician's song

The cotton laid in claim
covers rent in castle grounds
while thundered charges flit
tearing sky behind the clouds

The lavender was picked
for the mother of her birth
to quiet wilding wails
and restore a daughter's mirth

The chestnut threw her casks
as we scattered on the grass
and poppies sprouted free
for a window to the past

The bill o' fare was paid
for encounters with the mice
as ale was guzzled down
and a festival, enticed.

— Barry Hollow

Symphonies of the Wild-Hearted

—I stumbled on the drops of brandy—
Light spring breeze,
lets light springs breathe,
as bluebells bow for trees who prance;
these princes known to prance.

With gentle grace, the boughs bend knees,
while skipping past,
blissful, kissful, dancing trees
take these days now at steady canter,
and on this braw, blithe day
the longing of a summer's saunter.

- *Barry Hollow*

—Friendship circle—
Aussie bunch, Sunday, lunch
In shady nook, drinks we took
Meandering path, babbling brook
Following after, trekking; laughter
Summer, corn, path well worn
Cows, sheep, dung on feet
Nettles, trees, stingers, PLEASE!
Gentle breeze, birds and bees,
Roasting, wheeze, feels like 40 degrees!
Fence goes buzz? touch it? Does.
Memories, made, smiles in spades
Friendship, circle, what a miracle!

- *Barry Hollow*

―Murmuration―
I'm deep inside the pack,
soaring with elation
my kin swerve to and fro,
connected syncronation.
Sweeping, swooping pulses,
I float amongst the crowd
ritual and seasonal
over fields and through the cloud
random shapes and patterns
my acrobatic crew,
these stunning cunning stunts,
it seems to those who view.
Beating all together,
our unity is bound
I'm leading from the front
and our roosting place
is found.

- Barry Hollow

―Wee Finch―
Buffeted by many winds
And spray of wild seas
The finch sings of her story
And of homes in many trees

She sings of witnessed tragedy
Of vessels torn asunder
Dashed upon the rocks
By judicious raging thunder

She tweets of fun and frolics
Of companions by her wing
The times they danced together
When they joined to hear her sing

This finch tells of her story
Of those who shared her nest
Devotion shared between them
Giving each of them her best

This twilight song she sings
Becomes at once so solemn
She chirps her last
And from this branch, forever fallen

- Barry Hollow

Symphonies of the Wild-Hearted

—Effie & Jeff-ie—

Effie the Spider lies silent in wait,
To spring a big trap, no need for some bait.
Spinning her silk in a curious weave
And licking her lips for a treat to receive!
Now Jeff, the wee critter, wings this way and that,
off to the shops? From his hoose or his flat.
But nature is cruel and nature is fickle,
So beware, oor wee Jeff, you'll end up in a pickle!
He ducks and he dives and he dodges the net,
Revealed to him due to the dew and the wet!
So Effie goes hungry and Jeff is a-flight
This day is now his......the lucky wee.......shite!

- Barry Hollow

—El Toro—

this stunning mortal bull, resplendent
focussed on survival
fate already tied and dependent
on the prancing matador, his rival

mind state fixed, he's now transcendent
cape flares, waiting on his snorting arrival
darts and swords thrust, with no accident
leads him straight, to life deprival

- Barry Hollow

—Teeny tiny newt—

This teeny tiny newt, who lived in Lilliput,
wore a teeny tiny suit while she played a flouncy flute.
This teeny tiny newt looked awfully very cute,
as she whizzed right down the chute,
but she bumped her tiny tush on a teeny tiny root!
Although she didn't give a hoot, she scolded this poor root,
and while her flim was all in flam, a big and brawny brute,
stole in and took a pook, of her flimsy flouncy flute!
Speeding off now with the flute, he gave the flute a toot,
but his point was mostly moot, as you see he was mute!
Now the teeny tiny newt now began to give pursuit,
to retrieve her flouncy flute upon his rueful running route.

As we haven't quite yet said, of the big and brawny brute,
that his face was rather dapper and divinely quite hirsute!
So his long and lengthy tasche did topple and did tangle,
causing him a great fandangle as if mingled by a mangle!
This allowed the tiny newt to retrieve her flouncy flute,
from the hirsute and brawny brute!
As they stood just by a wood, unfamiliar with this mood,
in a powdered perfumed puff, there appeared a troubled troubadour,
from a secret silent wooden door.
He asked the newt to toot, on her flimsy flouncy flute,
the swiftly swivelled round to the hirsute and hairy brawny brute,
whom at once produced a lute.
So the trusty thrusty trio, sang some soulful silly songs,
as they bounced and bing-ed and bonged, as the trio trouped along,
But the star of this here story is the teeny tiny newt,
who came from Lilliput and wore a teeny tiny suit, playing proudly on her flute!

Symphonies of the Wild-Hearted

—New—

As brooding gaze is drawn by might
To neon magma glowing bright
And languid lava's latent lust
As fervour builds this fateful night.

This zealous plot it tests this trust
Through cloud of sprouting acrid dust
And lungs draw in this mantle fume
Near blooded Nature Mater's crust.

Behold Event Horizon's womb
Eruption bears new life from plume
And luminescent core is borne
Upon majestic lava's tomb.

Embrace new birth with absent scorn
As shadow smashed on this new morn
And Welcome Song through blasted horn
Of crater's swaddling blanket, worn

- Barry Hollow

—Autumn—

copper canopy
revealing wistful wisdom
with pure grace we fall

- Barry Hollow

—Air—

giving lift to wings
warmed by auburn aurora
as aeons unfold
this aria sustains all
to scintillate souls and fires

- Barry Hollow

—The beast from the east—

The Beast from the East is hungry,
She's dark, foreboding and angry,
Devours the landscape, eats up the pastures,
mountains and lakes, she has us in raptures!
She whirled and blew us, fierce & ferocious
No prejudice, bias, for the old or precocious,
attacking the flesh if you dare to expose,
the ends of fingers & frost bit your toes!
Jack-knife lorries & cars pirouette,
Pumping the brakes, it ends in regret....
Stock up on milk! Bread bought in panic!
The end of World & acting quite manic!
But here we are now, the Beast lost her roar,
Snow-people hats lying sad on the floor
All back to work & back to the drudge
No sign she passed through but a pile of sludge.
Goodbye wild storm, you gripped us then fled
But what do I do with this MOUNTAIN OF BREAD?!!

- Barry Hollow

−Plastic war−

Off to ocean, drastic waste,
finding out to where it raced,
detritus party of death-wrung piles
a-top the sea,
it stretched for miles.
Starbucks and Costa cups,
why share your drink with cute seal pups.
This blackened age of single use,
this plastic life is so obtuse,
micro beads for fishy feed,
mirror of our immoral deeds,
cotton buds and drinking straws
tangled in our turtle's jaws.
To save our planet, we have no time,
to rectify this guilty crime,
to stop this horrid vile pollution,
and work as one for absolution.
This transatlantic frantic plastic,
what we've done is not fantastic.
Warning needed to wake our minds,
or make our peace with dead whale finds
on littered shores and oily beaches,
as up our streams it surely leeches.
Now open eyes to make it clean,
this deathly float in our Gulf Stream
Films of birds and films of fish,
bathing in this dirty dish,
our dolphins swim with can dividers,
it needs to stop! Government deciders!

− Barry Hollow

― The yellow oak ―

This amber canopy, tall and proud
And roots connected, deep in earth
I spy a traveller on the ground
And pondering paths, they look around
And wonder, of which way has worth

My wooded wedge of brothers' stand
Dividing ways for pilgrim's progress
And bearing witness of this land
And keep an eye on what he's planned
But where he'll go, we've no second guess

What can't be seen of seasons past
Are fallen trees across those roads
For skipping forward far too fast
Will slow you up, by stark contrast
But standing still, progress erodes

The worthy traveller does not see
These ways are crossed behind the wood
And if they did they'd turn and flee
As hindsight's crystal clear for thee
Though journey's purpose, oft misunderstood

- Barry Hollow

L. T. Pelle

@l.t.pelle

L. T. Pelle is an American poet and yoga teacher. She has been featured in numerous poetry anthologies such as: *We All Breathe The Same Air*, *Steady Hands: Odes to Our Fathers*, *Mosiac*, and *Gratitudes: To Our Mothers*.

—Rivers & rivers & running—
in the deep soul
there is a river
& in that river
another sound
water rushing with swallowed reflections
& i, the spirit,
a song, a hush of roses
i go to the forest to forget my gardens
the corset of dreams
that hasn't yet breathed

— L. T. Pelle

— Birdsong arrhythmia —
somewhere in the woods
there's a neglected home covered in vines
in humming green and loose-leaf snakes
& she looks like a forest with eyes (our home)
she looks like the unspooling of this birdsong arrhythmia between us
and we'll run our hands along this verdant abode
feel it—
the texture of beginnings
the pleated tangents
cat-tongued and longing.
inside my mother's teapot collection
& your father's cigar boxes.
our old home
of warm bread and nostalgia
with the windows painted shut,
we leave the door open
for fresh air & welcome

— L. T. Pelle

—Interruption—
ask a child,
"what is the
sound
a shadow makes?"
and listen to the way they harmonize between wolf and bird...
having never heard
sky & soil
interrupt each other

- L. T. Pelle

—Where to find an always—
always:
in the little trees
in the worded warmth
& want & whys

- L. T. Pelle

Symphonies of the Wild-Hearted

—Escape as a breathing technique—

escape is a forest dream
a lilac hiding in leaves the nymph traded her petals for
for beauty is an incoherent poem
a pruned and trellised howl
    . and fragrance speaks louder than hiding
    . (and they'll turn her into music when they find her)
a flute,
another lovely hollow
with someone else's breath

— L. T. Pelle

—Forest one—

she is a forest
in a dream &
i think i recognize this tree this
feeling
of loving
of losting
& oh
how i love this
sheet wandering——walking
on the eyelid side
of the street

— L. T. Pelle

—Womb green—

mother was green
i saw her fields sea with green blades,
and yellow yellow with weedless joy
the ground was a
pointillism of her smiles

— L. T. Pelle

—Hush, hush—
i hear the adjectives in your silence,
like
the yawning welcome of zinnias
to the spring.

- L. T. Pelle

—Trees —
the trees,
they walk away in poetry
and what am i but a great stillness
playing footprints

- L. T. Pelle

—Orange grove—
it was the beginning of summer;
love's junely oranges
fell plumply along the groves,
like a yawn,
blooming out from your mouth,
from a dream—

- L. T. Pelle

Symphonies of the Wild-Hearted

—What the trees are pointing at—
scarlet oak
sweet birch & pine
your body of hands,
how does it feel to hold each season like a lover?
to borrow her clothes after you're done
a whole life spent pointing at so many things
your whole body saying,
"look, look"

— L. T. Pelle

—Wild er ness—
the forest had no walls
and yet it felt as if our skin ended there
as if every time we kissed
a door was locked behind us

— L. T. Pelle

—Rainsong—
god, give me prayers
drunk with worlds
and violet peonies
i want nothing more than wanting
for this is how you give grey weight to clouds

— L. T. Pelle

—The tree beneath my skin is called a splinter—
the tree beneath my skin is called a splinter
and if the birds have made nests with what i have left behind:
needles and pins and green barrettes with teeth
then am i not also beneath the skin of the forest?
can i claim some small song
robin egg
a blue hidden in the leaves
even if only the sleeping ones
and mother animals can hear it?
because i'm there.
just be/neath her skin
& i'm sorry about the pain
i just want to be felt
when you hold things

- L. T. Pelle

Symphonies of the Wild-Hearted

—My almost—
here it is, my almost
tormented as a spring
and april
with her shattered seas.
i offer you only a feral love
blackberry wine
and forestfloorfeathers
a howl
the wind laments—
and know that this love has not become a coffin
that you do not bury
what you release

— L. T. Pelle

—For the forest—
i am here to serve
whatever it is within me that
howls without echo
i am here to serve my wild er ness

— L. T. Pelle

—Laying/lying—
dahlias of another offering—
once again,
i find myself forgetting to believe
to sip on the sweet coconut milk of wonder
as if i was a newborn of the moon, and hungry
and what else are gardens for
if not for plucking?
for laying lilies and orchids at her feet?
to eat a bird
you must first remove her feathers—
to taste a goddess, too

- L. T. Pelle

— Nocturnes —

someone in the forest is carving our names into trees
while spring creatures herself into storms
nocturnes, questions,
knocking
the songs of the spilling
i never know if they're lessons or some kind of spell/ing
my words, the weeping bells
the blue and rainly larkspur
garden of black seed and footprints
who is the sound my lilies make
emulating the owl, the writer, the scientist
for *to pray* does not indicate god
but rather
to call upon new adjectives to pray with

— L. T. Pelle

—Leaves—

my stories

are back alley holy

temporary tattoos

of flowers we cannot name and i pick at them like wounds that color instead of ache

a black confetti of spells dusting down my arm

when she holds my

broom hand

when we kiss

our wands

are the first things

we undress—

unbuttoning

the

leaves

— L. T. Pelle

Symphonies of the Wild-Hearted

—The coyote & the buttercup—
once i was the hawk that stole my eyes,
but now
i am simply
the eyeless one.
& you ask me
why do i go to the garden
to replace these missing limbs, but where else is poison
made so beautiful?
& sure i am
just another
yellow trust-fall of poetry,
but i believe myself to be
the pouring
the buttercups have been waiting,
open-mouthed,
to catch.

— L. T. Pelle

—Within figs—

& with each passing day
my imagination carries to me these figs,
these found hearts
(violet & green & rotten)
full of seeds and treeborn:
words
they are a lover, who know
i like my flowers wasp-hearted and
edible.

— L. T. Pelle

— A craving —

i crave
your forest,
your forest,
your quiet
incarcerated trees
i want these bedsheets of moss and bone

— L. T. Pelle

—Untitled—

spring is a silken sorrow
a stemmed sigh
and when the blue finds me
dusking through the psalms
with cruel violets and vespers
with black currant calm and curses
   . i am a black current,
the dawn end of sleep.
lost as a tenuous dream, i dream
& when the forest is your altar
who else can lay upon it,
but the storm?

— L. T. Pelle

Symphonies of the Wild-Hearted

—Fate—

fate,
waiting like goosebumps
beneath my skin,
like my mountains
I do not climb, but become

— L. T. Pelle

—Welcome—

& let your welcome mat be the
ground between pine and promise
for somewhere
there is a tree
whose bark has grown over your story
like an ancient book
but it is not your job to find it,
instead
gather the needles and cones
and burn in your home
the scent of
unknowing
which is wisdom
which is wisteriaed & wanting
& wreathes
which you must hang from your door
in celebration of welcome,
in the shape of faceless clocks

— L. T. Pelle

Adeline Gray

@adelinewrites

A lover of all things literary, Adeline Gray has been enthralled with poetry since she first picked up a collection of the works of Emily Dickinson as a vacation souvenir around the age of eight. She is passionate about storytelling and writes poetry by narrating life inside her head and scribbling down images here and there. Adeline is a literature, composition, and creative writing teacher with a sweet, growing family that is her greatest joy.

Symphonies of the Wild-Hearted

—Everything—
dawn breaks,
flower petals crack open,
rocks fall into the earth.

a heron sips from a stream,
sunshine beams in glory,
glinting off the water.

a leaf uncurls for the first time
to smile at the clouds,
a bee finds pollen.

none of this means anything,
except that it is everything.

- Adeline Gray

—Beg the earth—
Soggy leaves stick to me with
watercolor raindrops,
my nails bleed, jagged with dirt,
I lay my heart to the ground anyway
and beg the earth to tell me
her secrets—

what came before,
what will be behind,
where are the lost treasures,
is there anything here to find?—

She says nothing,
so I dig deeper—fingers blue
and frozen.

- Adeline Gray

― A heart who never heals ―
Tell me there's something beautiful
about a barren tree branch
naked in the cold of winter
and not because it used to hold magnificent leaves
and not because spring will come again,
but because it exists—because it is beautiful.
Tell me there's something lovely
in discarded coffee grounds,
grapes fallen from the vine and trampled,
in an angry cry, a hollow scream—
things that can't be redeemed—
in anguish with no relief,
the catharsis that never comes,
the love unrequited,
an autumn leaf that won't crunch,
a floating fist, a door that sticks,
a broken window of colorless glass.
Tell me there's beauty in decay.
Tell me that a heart who never heals
can still be whole.

― Adeline Gray

Symphonies of the Wild-Hearted

—Considering the sea horse—
Is there a plug at the bottom of the ocean,
somewhere in the middle, maybe, and deep,
deep in the water so we can't find it?
Surely the sea creatures—bound
to be more trustworthy—
would leave it alone.

They'd swim about and know
not to spill their water to land.
And why don't I know any
better? Why am I always spilling
watery edges and pulling the plug from
the back of my eyeballs until my ocean is land
and my land sky, and I am not an I
or a me or an upright anything other than
an inside out universe with sand
on her kitchen floor and dishes for dunes?

I don't blow in the wind as
gracefully as seagrass, and the sound
of waves is far more soothing if I do not
make it myself,
but here we are,
me who isn't me and I who isn't I.

Here we are, alone together and considering
the seahorse who swam right on by.

— Adeline Gray

— Waiting for a tornado —
isn't about whether or not
destruction barrels through,
it's about moments when the sky
moves too quickly away from you,
threatening to rain down abyss
with a wink and cackle and swish.

It isn't about if the windows will break or
trees split or petals spill
or whether or not my heart will fall out of my chest
or whether or not I turned off the coffee maker
or whether or not you love me.

It's about the waiting,
sitting vigil for the tragedy that may not befall you,
preparing in stillness for what is yet to be.

It's balancing
knowing and not knowing,
knowing and not feeling,
feeling and not knowing—so

tell me it'll all be fine,
tell me the storm will break in time,
just know it isn't about you being right—
you could very well be wrong—

it's about holding my breath,
the purgatory, the uncertain death,
ribbons of inkling and premonition;
it's about the in between—
and waiting is hard for me.

— Adeline Gray

Symphonies of the Wild-Hearted

—A faded dream—

Forgive me if
I am a flower petal
wilting in your grasp;
my spine is often made
of broken stems
and sticky sap;
I am here today, in the wind tomorrow,
and to believe that anything in me could

hold

you

up

would be to put all your hopes in a faded dream,
a sepia-colored photograph with

worn

edges

that

might

crumble

when she's placed inside your pocket,
that you drop into a milky puddle on the corner of 57th and Oak
when you pull out a stick of gum as you

wait for

the light

to change

and leave behind for someone else to find

because it's

too

much

trouble

to save someone
who doesn't want to be found.

— *Adeline Gray*

—Heavy pebbles—

In the space of a held breath,
I wait for the prisms to come
and for the windows of my soul to be
cracked open with heavy pebbles
from the creek behind my grandmother's house
until enough of me has spilled out;

as of now,
even I cannot see myself,
even I cannot watch stones
skip over the water
and know whether or not it's me
who's been hit.

I am a walking wave
of the ocean, a fish
in waters deep
who can't escape the air,
and what is it I'm chasing, after all?

The shore is not far off, but I see the bottom;
I am stuck here
in the early middle of deep water
where it is light enough to seem like day
but not bright enough to breathe.

— *Adeline Gray*

―By the light of the yellow moon―
Too much, not enough—
my buried secrets find me in the yellow moon,
when the earth is still and the sky is dark
and my sobs are muffled by shower steam and
pillows; it is then in the quiet night
that my brain beats louder, and I close my eyes
to count the shapes on the ceiling again,
to recall the faces I see in the shadows above
me, free and floating while I lie pinned,
and I flip through the ceilings I've seen,
falling popcorn at my great aunt's house
that smelled a bit of mothballs,
Adam's hand to God's,
leaky ceiling tiles, exposed duct work, dust and cobwebs,
lines in a cathedral, accented with reds and greens and golds,
rain in my eyelashes, angels staring;
my arms don't reach far enough to pull me up
from your grasp—too much of you, not enough of me,
and will I float away eventually,
maybe under the soft light of the yellow moon?

- Adeline Gray

—Let the sea grow legs—
Let the sea grow legs, follow me
from the gray shoreline to a tree—
one wave, two wave, plant a seed
find out what you really need;
underneath this tree we'll lie
till the flower petals die—
Let the sea grow legs, follow me
from the gray shoreline to a tree.

– Adeline Gray

—Roots—
It's true that the roots reach farther underneath
than the branches above,
which means we're missing a piece—
the magnificence, the power,
the hard work of the tree is beneath.
The strength is deep and deeper still,
silent and secret screaming
just a world under our feet,

and I'd like to visit below the base of a tree
and see if maybe this is how it's been with me.

– Adeline Gray

—Leave me be or devour me whole—
I want to ride home
on the wings of a thundercloud
headed for the middle of the ocean
where there is no one
but the saltwater creatures
who will leave me be
or devour me whole,

and trust me
when I say
either would be
just fine.

— Adeline Gray

—Catch fire—

I want to walk across an icy corn field
barefooted and bleeding,
let the shards and flakes of snow seep
into my bones until they turn brittle.
Surely then they'd crack, snap, break,
and the rest of me wouldn't feel so lonely, so hollow,
so spilled out.

I think about Aunt Helen sometimes and
how she's losing her mind slowly
like misplaced keys on Monday
and an unattended lit stove on Wednesday—

life is like that sometimes;
you just need to turn on the flame to watch it burn
and wonder if by some miracle
you'll get to catch fire, too.

— Adeline Gray

—I need the water—

The sun stings
my already blistered skin;
watching the waves,
I bury my feet in the silky, scalding sand
to feel again, and I try my best to breathe in
more salt than air;
I crave it so desperately
as I watch the horizon stare back at me,
and I crave that too,
the great unknown behind the curtain of the sky.

The sand and the shore are fine for first moments,
but sharks be damned, I need the water and the waves;
I dive into them, bob up, and dive in breathlessly again;
I swallow gulps and gulps of air
and plunge to the ocean floor,
terrifying everyone but myself.
I want to swim to farthest sand bar,
make friends with the fish;
I am probably a sea creature
somewhere within, probably just
below the surface of my burned skin.

Mama says I am a mermaid,
but mermaids are too beautiful
and too human and too complicated;
I am an anemone or a starfish
or one of those mostly undiscovered ugly things
lurking in the bottom bottom bottom of the sea
where it's moonlight and inky water all the time;
I know this because mermaids long for land,
but I love the way the waves twist
me into them and me into me;
my organs churn in my belly,
and I am glad to swim in the depths
of fiery lungs and pounding heart;

back then it was many years
before I would read about Edna Pontellier,
but already I was dreaming of going that way;
already I felt more alive
the more I looked danger in the face;
the waves are the only place I am brave.

— Adeline Gray

—Let me drown—
Let the waves
roll over me
as I lie still
and breathless
on the shore.

Let icy glass
with foam lips
kiss me
up to my eyeballs
over and over until
my breath is not my own.

Let my eyes and my mouth
flutter and close in
rapid succession
as they fan the flames
in my dissolving lungs.

Let the frigid ocean thunder
baptize me as I beg
my heart to thaw.

Let me drown
so I can breathe
again.

— Adeline Gray

—The core of me—

I find hope in the stillness before a storm,
I know there is beauty in the hail,
I feel at home in the raindrops,
even when they flood together
instead of plopping gingerly on cool tin roofs.

I remember those gentle days walking along
the beach, hand in hand with my mother,
memories sugared over and glinting
in the sunshine and scalded into
my sunburned shoulders.

I find duality in the flattest of things,
and I seriously doubt I am as resilient as I seem;
I will bend, bend, bend and not break,
but I sense one more blistering wind will
be more than the core of me can take.

- Adeline Gray

Symphonies of the Wild-Hearted

—It is well with my soul—

I sit beneath a weeping willow
playing its leaves like a pipe organ,
humming the tune of my grandmother's
favorite old hymn,
carried away by a yellow breeze
of long forgotten words;
wrapped up in the shade
of this willow tree,
it all floods back to me, and
I trust my memories to the leaves,
soft shards of green glass.

I recognize her in my organ's pedals—
the far-reaching roots that start strong
and need more room than most
to roost and roam, to grow, to feel free,
but they hold their place ever so tightly,
grasping what they can reach—
the pieces of her I always wanted to be me,
only my roots are not so sturdy;
I spin off in weak places,
grasp too tightly to all the wrong earth,
and let go when I should be holding on for air—
I clutch the leaves, autumn cool in my hands
and remember the willow's need for water—
aggressive, immediate, so necessary for survival
there almost can't be enough—
and I sigh a smile and reconsider
how much of her is planted in me.

— *Adeline Gray*

—The sky at my feet—

I have looked too many times
and in too many places—
the clouds, my heart,
the waves, your hands,
the rain, those pills—
for answers
even before I'd
mustered the courage
to ask—to think up, even—
the questions,
and as it turns out,
that was my problem all along;

all I needed
was a rattle and a shake,
the sky at my feet,
to bring breath back
to my veins.

— Adeline Gray

—I am learning—
Eyes of flowers
planted tightly in corners
of a partially manicured garden
somewhere reaching for the sun
long for butterfly kisses
and cool summer mornings
before the dew has seeped
into the next day—

I am learning to hold the flutter
of my beating heart in my hands
instead of between my teeth.

Beneath my sternum,
you will find nothing
but a jar of sea water
on the warm side of tepid.

And that is fine, for I am learning
to let myself breathe,
to let myself see,
to let myself need.

— *Adeline Gray*

―Just what I need―

If I grab this branch like a maypole garland
and spin, will the world whirl
differently on its axis,
will my head and my heart
and my lungs come to calm?

Will the branches envelope me into
a member of their system—
a long lost cousin to the third stick from the bottom,
wishing everyone a good morning when the sun rises—

Will they hem me in until my breath is extinguished
and the sky goes cold and I grow leaves myself?
And will that restricted resurrection be just what I need?

Until one day far, far away or behind,
unknown because I've lost track of time,
a little girl with brown curly locks and a butter yellow bow,
handful of wildflowers and weeds,
comes skipping over the earth under me;
I recognize her bare feet, then
her giggles, the color of honey bees,
and I sing to her—yes, yes, little girl,
be free—and I feel certain she is me.

- Adeline Gray

—I'm not sorry—

I am not straight lines and sharp corners;
I am more of a circle with jagged edges,
and if that doesn't make sense to you,
it's okay—I am not only one thing.

At my core
I am a contradiction,
hard to pin down,
easy to figure out,
because I wear parts of my heart
on my sleeves and pass out
pieces of me like Halloween candy,
and it stings, it gets sticky,
but I'm not sorry.

The rest of me you'll
likely never see because
most people tire of digging deep
only for their progress to be destroyed
in the morning when my eyes
wake to the sound of shoveling dirt—
I am rarely afraid, but I do spook easy—
and I have decided that it's okay;
not everyone is meant to bury themselves
within me, and furthermore,
I do not have the room,
and I don't much care,
but it makes me awfully sad.

I am fall and spring in the same breath,
autumn leaves and blooming flowers;
it's possible now
that you understand me,
but it is more likely that you just think
you understand because this is a poem,
and a poem makes everything suddenly
relatable, and with this fact,
some of me sighs, and some of me smiles;
I am not straight lines and sharp corners;
I am a circle with jagged edges.

You may slice your fingers,
but you can hold me close.

— Adeline Gray

—Stand and bloom—
Lightning starts soft in the distance
after pounding thunder
and suddenly, violently,
he splits the bradford pear in half;

her arms tremble on the sobbing ground,
a tangle of regret and ache for moments
when the storm was yet far off,
but she will rise tomorrow;

though she will live maimed,
she will not be her wounds, for
she will s t a n d and b l o o m.

- Adeline Gray

—And so it is with us—
In the middle of an empty, dried up field,
where the earth is cracked and worn ragged,
a weeping willow thrives.
She stands alone,
a mirage in the desert,
the tired bouquet of fresh cut flowers
that should have withered last week
but somehow hangs onto fleeting life
as if the blue glass vase it sits in
is where it was always meant to be,
and so it is with us, I think,
staring at each other until we've made a gaping hole.

Lying under that tree,
we sing our secrets to the leaves,
lock eyes when night
fades to dawn;
I light a single leaf on fire
and watch the virus catch—
up first then side to side.
There's one way out,
but neither of us moves until the moment is gone.
We lie again—all wrapped up, that first
moment our pinkies brushed
a distant memory—
my head upon your shoulder,
I fall asleep to crackle of the flames
and the steady rhythm of your beating heart.

— *Adeline Gray*

Symphonies of the Wild-Hearted

—Of wind and water—
Your hands are wind
on the water of my eyes,
lacking depth by the afternoon,
low tide and waiting
for you to gaze through me
gently and without reprieve;

fold me to pieces between your fingers;

let your words spill over me as
stones skipping on the surface of water
begging to ripple;

hold me—I may be water in your hands,
but hold me;
hold me here.

— *Adeline Gray*

—Let me love you—
Sing to me sweetly
songs of the wind,
and I will recount
fairytales of the sea;

lie with me until caterpillars
dance across my ribs
and cocoon in your eyes;

and, I say, let the rain
come for us—we do not need
the cover of the trees—
let fat droplets bore holes
into our bones
and wash us away
into the rapids of the
mighty Mississippi
until we are battered
and broken but still
holding on;

rest with me in the riverbed
between a smooth pebble
and jagged sand.

— *Adeline Gray*

—If you let it be—
With the flavor
of indigo and elderflower
I can see the before, the after, even now,
and with the fragrance of lemon zest
the in-between lingers in the air,
and I wonder why you're so stuck
on the not-right-now—the magic is
waiting underneath
a tattered blanket of
rustling leaves in the fall,
and to hear it,
to see it,
to know it,
you need only to
wait.

Petals drop, a lizard loses his tail,
the sky flips over on its head,
we kick a rock down
a tired old path,
and the ocean makes love
to the shore with violent panting—

it was here already, waiting,
watching. It's us and it's them
and it's now—if you let it be.

— Adeline Gray

Symphonies of the Wild-Hearted

—I am too well hidden//this poem is not for a lover—

You won't find me inside myself—
I am too well hidden elsewhere
in grains of sand and the sea gull's beak;
I am all sky and ocean filled to the brim
with inky stars and flecks of the moon
she has given me that I might shine;
I don't always, but she tries.

Chilly on a summer's evening,
I will sit in silence with you
long until we try to speak and our voices
scratch because I know how
to be and be. My hands grow numb,
and my feet tingle from holding pens
and flipping pages; I am a busy body
with a busier mind until my bones smash
to dust and I can see flowers again.

I will stretch my veins over the neck of my
violin and play you a song, even if I don't
know the tune. I will see below
your skin that I might drink up your soul
until our hearts beat the same, our
spleens smile at each other, and
when your lungs feel like mine,

I will love you—
I will love you
past the end of time;
I will love you
when there's nothing left to find;
I will love you
when you've left me behind.

— Adeline Gray

Adeline Gray

—For now—

The air sweats into strips of cotton,
and I'd be choked if it weren't for the wind;
the fog had gathered
around the bellies of the trees until now.
It's falling down like raindrops,
gathering on my eyelids
while I draw shapes
and write these words in the dirt
instead of making my way home,
instead of washing the day off my face,
instead of making love to you,
instead of cooking dinner,
instead of asking about your day,
instead of pulling feathers that poke
out of the pillow case,
instead of filing my fingernail blue on
denim while you ask me where I've been,
instead of a hundred other things,
for now I am drawing shapes
and writing words in the dirt,
for now I am scraping off my fingerprints,
for now I am exchanging
the scent of you
for the breath of earth,
for now I am gathering fog on my eyelids
instead of leaving them open.

— *Adeline Gray*

—Petals like you—

The petals know nothing of when they will wither,
and I wish it had been that way with you, too.

I wish you would've kept your eyes closed
to the sun and let the rain have her way with you.

The petals know everything of the sun and the moon,
and this is how I think of you:

gravel roads in summer time,
words of ripe peaches,
eyes of muscadine.

The petals know nothing of everything
and everything of nothing, too,
and I wish it had been that way with you.

- Adeline Gray

@alanj.chambers

Alan J. Chambers was born in Wyandotte MI, but raised in Albuquerque, NM. He received his Bachelor's Degree in Accounting from the University of New Mexico because of his love for language and the connections it makes, especially within the world of business. He currently resides in Northwest Arkansas working in sales for the grocery industry. He grew up playing music with friends in Albuquerque in various bands in high school; his love for writing their music transformed into a love for writing stories. His childhood mutism and speech problems are minimized and he's sprinting after his dreams. In his free time, he likes to kick back, relax, and chill by a pool in the summertime while sipping on some pink lemonade.

Symphonies of the Wild-Hearted

—The fear of the cage my mother kept me in—

I'm sorry if my words made you bleed

For once
in my life
I wanted to think about what I
need.

Then I thought about the
next child
who didn't
feel
like they have a chance.

That's when I first rattled the caging-

I couldn't stop my
kneecaps
as they shook worse than
tremors in Arkansas.

'I just want to be free'

The words in my head
kept pounding
but I tried to filter my
threatening tongue

until small bursts
kept bubbling out

'I NEED TO BE FREE'

The cage burst open
I felt steel as it brushed
against my wings,

I bled
profusely.

But I still worried of you-
I hope you remember to worry of me.

Love,
your son.

— *Alan J.*

—Skeletons (it takes two to make a thing go right)—

I once fell in love,
but she had skeletons
in her closet.

Wicked, wiry, and weighing
on her-

I can remember the cringe
of my bones while
she savored
to share
her secrets.

I thought I could set them
upon my spine
to make her
better.

I didn't know
they'd drag me
screaming
into her closet,
only to become
one of them.

- Alan J.

Symphonies of the Wild-Hearted

—Perfect teeth (bright as summer)—
Cutting out any expectations,
 a small price to pay
for my miscommunication.

And yet, she said yes.

This thing called growing up
doesn't always bring you down.
Cause at 22
as she smiles
back at me,

I catch these feelings that I don't
know,
crawling towards my
face
making me smile
back at her.

My God,
My God,
My God,
She is,

beautiful.

I hope unlike the seasons
these feelings
don't come and
go.

— Alan J.

—The dancer's recital—
More than human
    when she twirls
        along the stage.

Her body an entire
orchestra,

        the keys
her tender feet seem to
know where to land
anywhere on the stage

        the strings
as precise as her
smile to the crowd
while they admire

        the drums
pumping with each
twitch of her muscle,
powerful beyond belief

        the brass
the drone of the audience
buzzing to a hum
as they treasure her

symphony.

– Alan J.

Symphonies of the Wild-Hearted

—Umbrellas & algebra (why is it you like me?)—

Is it the way
I always place
three sugar cubes
in your coffee?
Never two— still too bitter.

Or maybe it's
the way I
fascinate
over numbers
with a musician's
gusto.

Is it the way
I always guess
right, when we'd
need an umbrella?
Never mist— when you're around.

Or maybe it's
the smirk I
get
when I
see you in the
morning.

Is it the way
I always breathe
easier in this
world, with you?
Never lost— not with you.

— Alan J.

—For you, i'd be a lexicographer—
i felt dirty calling you
beautiful,
mainly because i know
there should be a better word for you

like,
bookish

with the way you
never notice
me,
when you drift deeper
into the pages
in front of
you.

- Alan J.

Symphonies of the Wild-Hearted

−Sweetheart (two-fourteen)−

My love tells me
that I'm much too
sweet,

but am I wrong to
assume,
it's what she wanted
when she asked for
us to be
'balanced'?
It seemed
sensible
for me to build, such an
equilibrium
to her
sour?

Because I'm much too
enamored
with the bitter
look of her
face,
as her rumpled
cheeks
crinkle deeper
when I do that
one thing,
that important thing,
that she's warned me of
time & time
again,

wrong.

You see the thing though
about my love's sour,
that keeps me coming
back,

is that it's not like the squeeze
of a
grapefruit
upon my chapped lips,

but more that crisp
swallow of air
that comes after a
lime

and just then
in those brief seconds after
when everything feels

good.

— Alan J.

—Sometimes we're all in need of firmer beds—
She stopped to ask,

"If I start to wear
glasses,
will you still get lost in my
eyes?

If I misplace my passion for
dance,
will you still admire me while I'm twirling between your
hands?

If I forget how to wake up and
smile,
will you still try to make the nighttime shine and bring me the
moon?

If I one day lose my
mind,
will you still crave to give me your
time?"

I stopped to answer,

'I promise to you,
to be the firmest of beds
you could ever dream on.'

- Alan J.

— (Speechless) in Washington—

the words crack me
as if the million
tiny strings attached to my heart
strumming our song
snap
leaving it to
drift
down
down
down
to somewhere deep within me,

i hope to relocate them someday.

but it won't be tomorrow.

she said she's
leaving to
seattle.

something about being
sleepless,
and her big
break.
it's left me
(tongue-tied).

— Alan J.

—The giant quiet (prickly as a peach) —
what if i never try to speak
again

will my lips chap up
and the words i think just
disappear

will it help to choke
out-

    this
lack of joy

what if i never try to speak
again

will my tongue dissolve
and any hope to get out
of bed stop

will it make my throat
doubt-

    why
it's even there

what if i never try to speak
again

- Alan J.

—Numb as a nectarine—
the floor as smooth
as the rind of a
nectarine,
it's holding me steady

while I watch the ceiling

the sweet nectar
of a summertime,
filled with her sunshine
is shriveling up

i hear something fall from a
tree outside

do nectarines
notice as
they dwindle away
in the winter?

- Alan J.

—Two a.m. (existentialism & you)—
as I lay awake,
at two a.m.

i find myself slipping into
a stupor,
    dripping past oblivion.

fake fragmented fractions,
instructing me
of how i feel
as they glow
against the wall-

    ¾ - i miss you
    ¼ - i'll be okay
    ¼ - this will never get better

these things don't add
up,
and i fear
they never will.

- Alan J.

—Mother (spring)—

still in pain

mother's
tea kettle shrieks

like a little one
sniffling for
chicken noodle

"rose hip tea"
mother corrects
the tune of
the porcelain healer

"you'll get over her soon"
reminded of a citrus
rose, as the liquid drifts
down my throat
alleviating some pangs

mother,
why do you believe
that the sun
will continue to
rise?
"Faith."

- Alan J.

—Father (time)—

father,
why does it feel
like the world
stops
when a part
of you leaves?

"the world didn't
stop, you were merely
out of breath."
I stop to process.
A little sigh,

makes it
lighter.
but what if that thought only
flickers til' it fades?

"then count up
& down
from six."

what does that
make you do?

"Release."

- Alan J.

―Stories―
Life
doesn't
start & stop
like the end
or beginning
of a book,

we just find our own scribbled
between
different middles.

― Alan J.

― Train stations (& maybes) ―

Turnstiles,
won't let me go back
to you
even if I still want too.

A woman swivels
inside the train-cart and
into her seat,
I'm reminded of you.

My heart
bubbles
as if I was going to talk
to you,
separated merely by moments.
I try to smear the froth
away from my chest
as I see she
isn't you.

The foam still seeps
through.

'Are you okay?
Did you meet someone
new?
Are you happy?
Did you get that big
break?
Are you traveling?
Did you see everything you
wanted?
Are you dreaming?
Did you learn to stop blaming
yourself?
Are you okay?'

Need to remember
this is just a stranger,

a red light flickers-
"Last stop before Apple Street."

she leaves
slower than you,
at least to me.

My heart settles-
as I vacate the train station
and this misery of maybe.

You're not coming home.

― Alan J.

Symphonies of the Wild-Hearted

  —You're only as good as your word —
  —(Perhaps that's why i'm always speechless)—

I screamed at the moon,
 she howled back
  "who are you?"

I don't know yet.
I just wanted to say goodnight,
moon.

I just found myself
crawling
or burrowing
deeper down a hole

I then saw the rabbit.

He left me around 8-
 that number that doesn't end
  just like the promise of summer nights.

I just found myself
drifting
or following
him down that hole

I need to get back to the rabbit.

I thought he came back at 13-
 that number that scares me
  did it mean I'm grown up?

I just lost myself
stumbling
or twirling
clumsily down that hole

I need to accept he's gone, that rabbit.

I thought I let him go at 21-
    that number that I waited for my whole life,
        now I wonder if it will ever come back?

I can't stop myself
contorting
or writhing
helplessly down that hole

I need to chase away the hauntings of that rabbit.

I tried to revive him at 29-
    that number where I realized I can't stop
        the days from spiraling away.

I just wanted to say goodnight,
moon,

So,
I screamed at the moon,
    she howled back
        "you are no one."

I'm running out of time, but again,

I just find myself
crawling
or burrowing
deeper down a hole.

- Alan J.

—Braver in Berlin—
Built to break walls,
but what will break me?

I reflect on the walls
that I climbed to get here,
just to find
another wall
in Berlin.

Though this one's
crumbled,
it's still cold and firm
against my fingertips.

I fear the wall waking.
The concrete walls
coming together
piece by piece,
blocking me off from
where I came.

I reflect, as I stare from
top
to
bottom,
on how many walls
never came down.

If not me
than someone else,
will break those.

- Alan J.

—The pursuit of (everything but) happiness—

what if my whole life
is just this
high-school track,
mundane & rounded
and I convince myself
that life will never be better than
the four years
that I didn't enjoy
stuck in this loop?

i pick up the pace

will growing old be as clasped
around my throat
as the feeling of when my legs contract
as I find myself circling this
high-school track,
what if I find myself
chasing everything
that won't make me
believe in the need to
breathe,
do I lack direction?

my breath gets
heavier,

as I round the corner of this
high-school track,
I start to wonder
if I can be
anything I can dream?

but I fear that maybe
I'll be
too focused on this
loop
& will chase
everything but,
(happiness)

the sun goes down

and the lights go on, at this
high-school track,
did I go too fast?
did I waste my time?
could I ever have done enough?
I round the last corner
and keep running
past these fences

I'd say to home,
but something about these paved neighborhoods
makes me want to pursue a way
to feel more than just okay

- Alan J.

Symphonies of the Wild-Hearted

—Water falls—
—(fearless as mr. jones)—

Dulled rocks
against my feet,
as I stare

below.
Red debris and water
blend as everything swirls
fifty feet down.
A fear of heights?
Definitely.

The world seems impossible
    when you stand   "He's not going to jump!"
        above it all.   'Need a moment
            to breathe.'

Will I jump?
Or just flop?   Gravity doesn't exist
        as I watch
    the tips of my toes
        break free from the ground.

Fifty. I feel so alive.
    Forty. Life is beautiful.
        Thirty. I close my eyes.
            Twenty. Love is this moment.
                Ten. I've been falling for a while.

Zero. Water fills any remaining fear in me.

— Alan J

—I can't find where the sidewalk ended—
—(an ode to childhood)—

I missed the point
        past where the sidewalk ends

and now I can't tell
where I'm at,
or going.

My heart starts
to beckon
for more
as I make a sound
like I'm wanting to go
'home'

What if I'm nothing more than these shots?
        Dripping down off the kitchen counter.
What if I'm just waiting for God?
        Maybe, he wanted me to do more than wonder.

I feel alone,
        yet surrounded
                am I setting myself up to fail?

Cause this world won't open up to me
        as I feel myself
sinking lower and lower.

I didn't even see the point
        from where the sidewalks starts

— Alan J.

Symphonies of the Wild-Hearted

—The man with the many pretty masks—
I'm not happy
    I just feel closer to joy behind the
        masks that let me hide
any other emotions from
cracking on my face.

I'm not sad
        I just like to grieve
                in rhythm with the rain
cause it makes me feel at one
with my blue as we pirouette.

I'm not mad
    I just breathe
        heavy, when life
wraps it's weight around my
chest to bring me down.

I'm not ashamed
    I just feel sorry
        about everything, even
the things that aren't actually my
fault.

I'm not afraid
    I just dread
        losing all of these
masks,
and letting everyone see,
me.

I'm not happy
    I just want to be seen
        as more
            than so sad
                all of the time.

— Alan J.

—Sad in London—

What if I'm as lost as the
face of George Washington
on a quarter,
in a London Heathrow
donation container, spinning down
the drain?

Two hours to a
twenty-four hour
plane ride home.

There's the sound of a coin circling
around the plastic,
whirling like a fabricated wind.

Not where I'm supposed to be,
or is that 'who'?

I don't think I'll feel like me,
will my life take me back?

The little boys eyes grow wide,
the end is coming soon.
He's American.

A little boys face stained
against the container,
waiting for the quarter to stop
and drop to the bottom.

Acoustic strums and airline beeps
to guide me back,
I'm not ready.
I'm not ready.
I'm not ready.

A jangle of coins finding their place,
though mismatched, hits the little boys eardrums.

The little boy walks away.

- Alan J.

Symphonies of the Wild-Hearted

—Life like a new york minute—

"Aren't you just passing through"
I'd say grazing by.

Taking in the
World
around me.

There's more faces than
milliseconds to a minute.
Passing me by like mid-morning trains
in this airport.
I want to know their stories,
and their smiles.

Would they want to know mine?

"Boarding for Flight AA 2161 to Boston"
I stare down at my watch,
the gold lettering filling my eyes.

My only wish with time,
is that I had enough
to hear all of those stories.

We're all strangers
boarding this flight.

I guess this life's like
a new york minute.

— Alan J.

—Free (seven-four)—

I want to feel as free
as a runaway
balloon,

fluttering through
the sky on
the 4th of July
as the fireworks
take off,

hoping to finesse
my way thru
the formulated
booms & crackles

threatening to end
my joy ride,

as the pressures
around me
fluster the

surrounding air,
the oxygen
& everything inside of
me

are being dared
to become one,
though that may
make it easier for me
to breathe,

but as I weigh
the burdens of a balloon's
blind ambitions,
I suppose,

there is a different freedom
to being human.

— Alan J.

Symphonies of the Wild-Hearted

—Tulips on the counter—

To the one that reminds me of a tulip-

what if I
sit you down,
on a counter
in a white room

and tell you
everything?

Would the walls
turn rose-red
when I tell you
you're the one
I've written
every love song
about
since I was like
8?

Would the walls
turn blood-orange
when I tell you
I want every single
second of your
youth?

Would the walls
turn tulip-yellow
when you see
the energy
pinching out of my
cheeks,
when I tell
you about the plans
I've made
for our future?

Would the walls
turn seaweed-green
when I layout
the maps
I have us
walking down
when we're both
102?

Would the walls
turn caramel-brown
when you
flip your hair
and my heart
skips?

Would the walls
turn seafoam-blue
when I think
of if I
never told you
any of this?

Would the walls
turn plum-purple
when you don't
know what to
say
and I
understand?

Would the walls
stay daisy-white
when I let you
go and learn
that
that's okay?

— Alan J.

— A cloud in the shape of a shel(l) —

I want to breathe as easily
as a collapsing lung
smoking on the cigarette
that will finally make him quit,

I suppose if he had though-
I would never have seen
the clouds
he formed.

Boats, trees,
and trampolines
among all of the
other things
that I was able to
see him wonder
drizzling from his
pen.

Maybe he'd think
I'm lame, and plain
and I actually believe
that'd be okay.

Because he still gave me
a dream,
and it lifted me
                    away
from the things
that crawled out
of my head
and taught me
fear.

In a stormy world,
he taught me to turn clouds
into whatever you believe.

— Alan J.

−Sun (flowers)−

hi. hey. hello.

Today I woke
up,
and didn't feel
like
a speck of
dust.

hi. hey. Hello.

Today I went
outside,
and didn't think
I was entirely
alone everywhere
I went.

hi. Hey. Hello.

Today I came
home,
and didn't want
to run a
thousand miles
to you.

Hi. Hey. Hello.

Tomorrow I will
grow,
and I'll wake
up
to smell the
sun (flowers).

− Alan J.

—There seems to be something in the stars—
—(oh wait... it's just your eyes)—

My dear,

we are the
pioneers
of hidden locations
and bent cartops,

I'd travel miles & miles
everyday
if that's the price for you to keep that
smile.

And whenever night draws near,

I wonder the
midnight phrases
I could say,

that will make you stay
as you lean in
closer

because as I look up at the stars,

I can't help but
ponder,
how they captured
such a similar glimmer

as they spiral
our lives,
like the iris
of you,

my dear.

- Alan J.

—The grand design of joy—

I hope I
become famous
and change the world with the way
I run this stage,
but if not,

I hope I
star alongside
the best, and am everyone's second favorite
fiddle,
but if not,

I hope I
sing some great songs
and get featured in the end
credits,
but if not,

I hope I
man the camera,
and am rewarded at some award show
no one watches
but if not,

I hope I
am the one who hosts that
show, and people love the
venues I built
but if not,

I hope I
make the best
food and they ask me
to serve the next show
but if not,

I hope I
make enough serving
and get to brush elbows with the stars
while supporting a family
but if not,

I hope I
still have the love
of my little ones
and they believe in themselves
but if not,

I hope I
get them angry, and they're inspired to be
better than me
and they find some real love
but if not,

I hope I
get a visit from them
when we're all old
and lonely
but if not,

I hope I
have nice dreams,
that get me through
some bad spots
but if not,

I hope I
find a little sunshine
and get at least one day to
breathe
and I'll always treasure that moment of joy.

— Alan J.

−Coming home (late eleven)−

I was told,
there's a place you can go,
a location called home,
but maybe it's only real in your
brain

the train doors
close
as I watch from my
middle seat (as I prefer
the balance) alone, tucked
closest to the door-
where I always sit,
just in case,

I mostly doubt that there's a
place that feels like
a home,
but there are these
moments,
these sunshine seconds,
where I can sense
a bright yellow path
leading to a door,
though I'm sure I'd steer elsewhere-

The rush of
friction,
as the train takes off
causes me to stir
about, blending my mind
with the real world,
I realize then
we're one & the same-

the train & this attraction with gravity
my self & this fascination with fantasy,
with our careless affinities
for self-control
but what if we were to lose
a few bolts?
there's a violent
crunch
as the train comes
unhinged
the colors of the train
blur,
like squinted eyes
after midnight,
the reds of the billboard ads go first,
as I ponder if life has enough
to get caught up with,
then,
the greens of the women's coat & her
tea, as both fumble
for some type of security

Symphonies of the Wild-Hearted

but chairs & cups do not care
when laws are in action,
then,
the blues of the conductors dress & hat swirl
with
the grays of the seat
he is clinging on to
as remorse for
what he could have been
helps his fingers let
go
yet I feel only
yellow,
though the shades are
unclear,
a battle of sun rise or set
as the discord cause my eyes
to blink,
as we brace for impact, our
joyride
comes to an end,

but this is all in my
head,
as I guess my real fear
is that I'll go back home,
states away,
& I will have no one to console
me in the times when
I too feel
unhinged.

The train continues
on, with
the reds of the billboard ads
reminding me that there's purpose
outside
of just glitz & glamour,
then,
the greens of the women's coat & her
tea, both swirling
either in chair or cup-
let me know that someday,
I'll find something to
settle into,
then,
the blues of the conductors dress & hat
highlight
the whites of his teeth
as he smiles upon
me, happy to be
alive.

I don't know
when or where,
nor with who
but someday,
I'd like to come home.

— Alan J.

Emily May Portillo

@poetry.on.the.exhale

Emily is a poet, mother, and avid over-thinker from the Boston area. She enjoys long walks to nowhere in particular and her children's smiles, because there's nothing that fresh air and love can't soothe. Most succinctly, she could be described as half wonderer, half wanderer, half headstrong humanitarian, and half hoping you noticed that was too many halves.

Symphonies of the Wild-Hearted

—Winter is here—
i need air.

february cold drifts in through the open window,
kisses my cheek.
my toes curl.
my lungs unclench their fists.
i am shaking hands and acceptance.

the snow is gathering steadily on the windowsill.
i do not move to clear it.
cannot move to clear it.
i have misplaced my feet.
my consciousness.
i am hardly even here.
i am only inhale.
only this ache.
only closed eyes and curved spine.
a body braced for the shatter.

let the snow build.
it only wants to warn me
that the storm is coming.

i don't have the heart to tell it,
it's already here.

— Emily May Portillo

−Autumn−

we are falling / do you feel it? / and i / am trying to hold ~~you~~ / hold ~~us~~ / hold on / like autumn / all gold and scarlet / and ~~dying~~ / and devastatingly beautiful / you / are so *beautiful* / i hope / i said that enough / i hope you listened / love, do you smell that? / the crisp ~~end~~ / the crisp air / there is something oddly / delicious / about what is fleeting / about what ~~will not stay~~ / about what cannot stay / ~~you~~ / we / were my favorite season / warmth / made of peonies and promises / but, now / it has grown / so cold / here / i wrap the memories / around my neck / ~~an infinity scarf~~ / a scarf / unraveling / coarse wool that scratches / reddens the skin / i am wading through / all the leaves / you said you would turn over / i have turned us over / and over / in my mind / but, it seems ~~you~~ / it seems ~~i~~ / it seems we / were never meant / to survive / the frost

- Emily May Portillo

—Timeline—
this day
has lasted
a lifetime.

has held furiously
to the grandfather clock's ticking hand,
like a loop of winter's sweater
caught on springtime's fingernail.
unraveling.
like summer
clinging to autumn's leg.
unwilling
to be left behind.

and i have spent
every second
reaching blindly
into the backseat of yesterday,
searching, desperately,
for a reason to believe
tomorrow
will be beautiful.

— Emily May Portillo

—Changing winds—

change is coming for me
like a summer storm.
i know
because there are cicadas
living in my belly.
they have chased away
every butterfly.
have driven out the fluttering
with their dramatic drone.

now, all that remains
is a low hum of heat.
a wildfire warning.
a steady buzz of beware.

my heart
is rubbing two sticks together,
eyes hungry for a spark.
she hasn't mastered it yet,
but she is persistent.

one of these days,
this tired body
will fill with flame,
and i am terrified
i will not survive
the burn.
will not live to see
the beauty
that is promised from the ashes.

- Emily May Portillo

Symphonies of the Wild-Hearted

—Overcast—

this morning
the sky
wears a tight-lipped smile.
the kind that doesn't reach
the eyes.

i tell it
it's alright,
you are beautiful
in every light.

i do not say
that i long for the azure sound
of its belly laugh.
the way its breath stirs my hair,
smells of hope.
i do not mention
how i miss the way it crinkles its nose.
its joy glittering in the sunshine,
as light as the wispiest clouds.
or that it has the sweetest dimples.
the prettiest teeth.

no.
i simply settle beneath it.
wait.
everything passes,
i whisper.

everything passes.

— Emily May Portillo

—Balance—
the petals fall from the dogwood
until the grass is a scent-stained sea.
beautiful bloodletting.

i press my palms firmly against the
windowpane.
bones heavy as graveyard dirt,
i exhale.
watch the window fog over.
watch the world outside
disappear.
i remind myself this is just
life.

endings and beginnings
chasing each other's tails.

there is a hummingbird in my chest.
she is wondering where i left
the sugar water.
why i am always either empty
or overflowing.
she bats her wings against my ribs
as if to say,
*i know you have not yet mastered moderation,
but, love, it will come.*

i am learning that it's all
a balancing act.

nothing is forever.

and, after all,
isn't that the meaning
of harmony?

– Emily May Portillo

-Self-portrait-

two eyes, piercing,
the color of the sea.
(gifts from my mother).

a mouth, with a voice
to be carried on the wind.
(some days, i am certain
it has wings).

hair, dark
like the richest soil.
long.
(from years of reaching
to root).

shoulders strong,
thighs stronger.
(from years of running
from rooting).

wide feet,
capable hands.
(my father's
before they were mine).

skin, loyal.
sun-loving.
soft and determined.
(flexible,
forgiving).

bones, stubborn,
with an invincibility complex.
(unafraid of sticks and stones
and words that wish
to break them).

mind, noisy.
kaleidoscopic.
(mad and messy).
storm-wild, sassy,
but beautiful,
nonetheless.

heart, steady.
(most days),
open.
(overly so),
resilient,
(resilient),

resilient.

— Emily May Portillo

Symphonies of the Wild-Hearted

—An alternate universe—
in which the early hours are lazy.
are spent slowly, softly, sweetly,
with my elbows resting on the edge of the sink.
the waking sun stretching its arms through the window.
lilac breeze, cinnamon sugar toast,
and the coffee pot, never much for mornings,
grumbling to itself on the countertop.

in which the prayer plant did not die,
and i do not spend my days
wondering
whether it was due to too much sunlight
or not enough.
whether i am
too much
or not enough.

in which i can sit on the shore of my favorite lake
in autumn, at dusk,
and life is not a broken record.
does not repeat itself where it is scratched.
does not repeat itself where it is scratched.
and the call of the loon
is all that haunts me.

here, your heart didn't go
(wherever it went
when it went).
or maybe it did,
but it learned to read the stars.
brought a map, a compass.
a pocketful of me.
found its way back.

here, my heart is not
a naked thing
on a broken fire escape.
shivering from more than just
the cold.
afraid of both the flames
and the fall.

- Emily May Portillo

—My lonely—

this / is my lonely / a summer town in winter / sun gone to find / a new lover / laughter always downwind / i am / a log cabin / quaint / inviting / but not built to withstand / the cold / abandoned / windows boarded against curious eyes / please, love / be curious anyway / be nimble fingers / patient hands / pry away the planks / clear the dust / wipe the grit from the mirrors / tell me / i'm lovely / even / in this most unflattering light / lift my chin to the sky / and remind me / they are only clouds / the sun never truly goes / the breeze is wispy wanderlust / too restless / to stay in one place for long / it will dance its way back to me / there will be laughter in these halls / warmth on this skin / again

- Emily May Portillo

—What will remain—

I. these blinds that never close quite right. the whisper of golden morning light through their crooked teeth. the amber warmth on my skin.

II. the creak of these floorboards. these bones.

III. stargazer lilies.

IV. the summer rain smile of the old scottish man behind the pharmacy counter. his puddled eyes when he tells me of glasgow.

V. chocolate. all of it.

VI. two sets of small hands willing to hold my heartbeat any time it gets too heavy.

VII. campfires. their soothing smoke and crackling laughter. their arms waving light to the sky.

VIII. the hole worn in the hem of my softest tee shirt. your scent on the collar. sandalwood, cedar, and sunsets.

IX. the towering oak in the backyard. its blanketing shade. its grandmotherly voice singing the breeze through my hair.

X. your memory.

XI. the hurt. forever, maybe. and that's okay.

XII. hope. that sweet, feathered thing.

XIII. me.

XIV. me.

XV. me.

- Emily May Portillo

—Gravity—

    what if
    g
    r
    a
    v
    i
    t
    y
    let me go?
let me
d r i f t   e t e r n a l
    on the back
of the unburdened breeze?
    would i find
    p e a c e
in the open air?
is there
    f r e e d o m
    there?

— Emily May Portillo

—Stay—
if i stand here long enough,
resisting the temptation
to flee,
tell me, will something
beautiful
take root?
reach down through the soles
of these restless feet
and anchor me
in the soul
of something greater?

darling,
i have never trusted
- anything -
long enough
to find out.

- Emily May Portillo

Symphonies of the Wild-Hearted

—Sometimes—

sometimes, i snap moments in half
just to see
if they will become more fragrant,
like parsley.
to see if they have
a sweet, caramel center.
if they might melt in my mouth.

sometimes my mouth feels like an ocean.
endless and uncontrollable.
words spilling, crashing, overflowing,
as if it will gladly offer
everything in me
for a chance to make love
to this world.

sometimes this world
does not seem to love me back.
it ties me to my solitude,
sets me afloat,
gives me a push.
leaves me to be an island
with no bridge to its distant shore.

sometimes, i build bridges
to other people
just so i can burn them.
let the flames seduce the ache.
let the woodsmoke
hold me like a blanket.
bury itself in my hair.

sometimes, i bury pieces of myself
in places i know i will never remember.
the redwood forest, the deserted playground.
i call it buried treasure.
search for bits of myself
as if this is only a game.
i am often in the last place i look.

sometimes, i look for joy
in soulless things.
there are days
i can almost convince myself
i have found it.
but, joy has a heartbeat.
cannot live
where love does not.

— Emily May Portillo

—Between the stars—

what is in the s p a c e   between the stars?
i want to send all my worries there.
all my stresses,
         anxieties,
              fears.
watch them
      flutter up
  ache by ache
like so many fireflies.
let them

     s o a r

into the evening sky
and be (cradled)
in the   void   between the glow
until they
     burn a w a y.
until they are nothing but
   dust
g l i t t e r i n g in the starlight.

i want to turn this
   pain
into something of
        beauty.
it would truly
be something to behold.

        ethereal.

— Emily May Portillo

Symphonies of the Wild-Hearted

—Drop by drop—
next time it rains,
leave the window open.
watch it gather on the sill
d
r
o
p by d
        r
        o
        p.
listen to the way each new arrival
honors a moment of quiet.
notice how patience is held
in the palm of the patter.
    b r e a t h e
through the in between.

remember, sometimes
this
is how change comes.

bit by bit.
easily missed.
beautiful and blushing
and then *gone*
before you're ready.

— Emily May Portillo

−Release−

the sun rises over the trees.
singshouts a scarlet and lavender *good morning*.
stomps warmth into the sleeping earth.

the wildflowers yawn, upturn their faces.
the lake stretches and waves.

and here, i sit.
my legs curled beneath me,
dew-soaked and honey-heavy.

i am so much aching humanity.
too much.

but, dawn has the softest touch.
the water is a kind-eyed woman.
and if nothing else,
i know this hour to be holy.

and so, i wait.

    for the moment
when the light slants its magic
just right.
dances its golden fingers
through my hair.
sweeps a piccolo prayer across
my skin.
whisks away my weariness
and whispers,
today
is a new day.

and when it comes,
i will trust.

let the wind cradle me,
a wounded wayfarer,
and waltz me to the sky.

release the hurt and
the hurt and the hurt

and gather the healing
in the endless blue.

— Emily May Portillo

—Reclamation—
some days
i wish nature
would take us back.
take all this blood,
all these bones,
all this ungrateful breath.
climb up our cocky limbs
like ivy,
until we can see the world
only
from between its leafy fingers.

make this mess of us
remember
where we came from.

make us wonder
how
we ever forgot.

— Emily May Portillo

— Dandelions —

i saw a dandelion
give itself over to the wind
when it could no longer bear
to be called
weed.

i watched
as it forfeited
all the pieces of itself
it was sure it needed.
let them scatter in the field,
not realizing
its sacrifice
would build an army.

there is no shame,
my love,
in giving in.
but do not mistake
giving in
for giving up.

do not confuse
sacrifice
for surrender.

weed
is just another word
for warrior.
so, next time you're told
you're growing like one,
stand tall.
tell them
how strong you are
in your softest sprouting.

show them
your wild
is wondrous.

- Emily May Portillo

—Irene—
there is a version in which the hourglass

doesn't topple. in which you know my face
beyond its breaking. in which you do not

grow hollow and we have *nothing but time.*

there, we sip chamomile tea side by side,
and you tell me of home. you remember

the joy of oranges. sweet enough to

make you forget the bitterness of war,
if only for a moment. there, you can still

picture the grace of the endless green, rolling

as far as the eye can see. you sigh and say,
love, you don't know peace until you've walked

barefoot through those fields, and you know that

i believe you. there, your gnarled hands are
warm and steady. your voice is clear and decadent

as birdsong, so much life curling itself contentedly

into each honeyed vowel. there, the only thing
standing between you and the world you hold most dear

is the atlantic, and oceans are not so vast, after all.

there, your mind is a handful of marbles. you hear
them clacking as you go about your day, and you

do not mind the racket. you're simply grateful not

to have lost them.
and, oh, so am i. *so am i.*

- Emily May Portillo

Symphonies of the Wild-Hearted

-The living-

everything around me
is so gracefully
   a l i v e,
even the emptiness
breathes.

speaks.

tells me
   h u s h l o v e,
your chaos echoes
            echoes
                echoes
                    echoes
here.
it does not belong.
give it wings.
set it free.

trust.

exhale.

i quiet my mind
long enough
to listen.
steady
my frantic heart.

i hear the
nothing
that sounds a lot
like peace.
the nothing
that holds the endless noise
in its pulse.
that offers, tenderly,
to hold me, too.
i decide
i would like to be
   a l i v e
like that.

i weave the silence
with its beating heart
into a basket.
bring it out into the sunshine.
begin collecting
open air,
birdsong,
springtime.

freedom.

— *Emily May Portillo*

—Twilight—

he is skipping stones,
chin high, back tall.
his brother is collecting pebbles in his pockets,
pants sighing, smile wide.
i am resting somewhere behind
on a moss-covered log.
quiet, comfortable,
content to fade into the landscape.

the sun is low
and everything is
soft soft soft.

soon, the moon
will wrap her jacket around our shoulders.
kiss us each tenderly on the head,
send us home, hand in hand,
with the crickets to sing us to sleep.

but not yet.

there is no moment
quite like twilight.

no sound
quite like the yawning earth.
all her muscles relaxing
into the glittering gray.

no sight
quite like the fledgling starshine
unfurling its blanket,
featherlight on their skin.

so, i hold this moment
beneath my tongue.

savor it.

sweet and smooth
and dissolving
so quickly.

— Emily May Portillo

Symphonies of the Wild-Hearted

—The only way i know—
i want to teach you
calm,
if nothing else.
how to be here.
how simply being
can be a ceremony.

but, darling,
you
are fast-moving
cotton candy clouds.
all sweet and swift
and shifting.
chasing the horizon
and thumbing your nose
at all my stubborn stillness.

you are not meant
to be pinned down.

not now.

and so,
i lift anchor.
put my finger to the wind.
stretch my skin into a sail
and gather as much of your breeze
as i can.

this
is how i teach you
to trust
yourself.
this
is how i learn
to do the same.
this
is how i hold you
while letting you go.

this
is how i love you.

with all the vastness
of open sea.

— Emily May Portillo

—When it wants to feel human—
you stop to tell the leaves
you like the way they dance.
my foot, restless, begins to tap.
i quickly glance down at my watch.

we need to get home.
there are so many things that have to be done.
(there always, always are).

i steady my breath and look up again,
and —
exhale.
the sunshine is smiling on your cheeks
as you whisper secrets to the wind.

you are wonder.

today, i do not rush you.
today, the rest of the world
can wait.

oh, love,
there is time for this.

this,
now,
is what joy looks like
when it wants to feel human.

like you.
your pint-sized frame
bubbling over
with all this endless april sky.
your bright, beautiful eyes
holding hands with mine.
your singsong voice,
clear and weightless,
chirping
mommy, look at me.
mommy, look.

mommy.

- Emily May Portillo

Symphonies of the Wild-Hearted

—Kanasatka—
we are bathrobe clad and barefoot
as we wend our way down the unruly path.
over and around the tree roots
in a dance i have known
for as long as i can remember.
i am five, with sand between my toes
and my big sister by my side,
and life has never been sweeter.
the resident ducks leave the safety of the lake
to waddle nonchalantly toward us on the shore.
i have given them all names
and am unfazed by their indifference when i address them.
i know they have been waiting for me.
(or at least, for over-large chunks of bread
to fall from my chubby fingers.)
i crouch down to coax the sassiest of them into my lap,
and i count.
five ducks, i think. *five, like me.*
today is a good day.

still in their pajamas, and armed
with a stale loaf and leftover pizza crust,
my boys, it seems, have claimed this idyllic place as their own.
unknowingly surrounded by soothing echoes
of the happiest days of my childhood,
they are at home here.
ducks drift lazily toward the beach
as the fog lifts equally lazily from the water.
my oldest, now five, hurls half-slices of bread

in what could only generously be considered
the approximate direction of the ducks.
he hasn't quite mastered the art of animal flattery
(or personal calm, for that matter),
so none venture close enough to nip at his hand.
meanwhile his brother, just one, dips the pizza crust in the sand,
(for texture, surely),
and aggressively shoos away any creature audacious enough
to hint at wanting a bite of his morning snack.
a chuckle bubbles up from my belly
as i sit at the old, peeling picnic table
that was once my mother's favorite perch.
today is a good day.

i say a silent thank you
to my lake
for all she has given me.
for how she has never asked
for *anything*
in return.

smile,
as her gentle waves
nod in understanding.

– Emily May Portillo

Symphonies of the Wild-Hearted

—Gratitude—

today, i give thanks.

for the bright morning call
of the chickadee.

for creaking floorboards beneath my feet.

for the smell of coffee,
and the quiet comfort
of coffee rings on tattered notebooks.

for roman numeral clocks
whose ticking hands are always gentle
(no matter how close i cut it).

for rickety porches that refuse to fall.

for the warmth of the sun
and the crisp chill of the breeze.

for buttons that have not gone missing.

for socks that do not slide down.

for small hands in mine
(even when they are sticky).

for leaves that crunch beneath my feet,
watercolor the broken sidewalk.

for the music of open sky.

for the way music looks so lovely
laid flat into words.

for the way words
feel like home
when little else does.

for a place to give thanks
for simple joys,
and for people, like you,
who hear me.

— Emily May Portillo

Emma Blas

@emmablaspoetry

Emma Blas lives near Gijón in Spain. Her poetry explores transitions, shifts of phase and form in the natural world of the Asturias, and the crossing points between the physical, psychological and imagined states of life on the Cantabrian coast.

Symphonies of the Wild-Hearted

—Poetry is—
the whisper of midnight jasmine
tracing the edge of a lapping breeze;
air cooled by the shadow of oaks,
crepuscular rays cast
in the hazy winter sun.
humus laced with the musk
of stalking beasts, crisping mulch,
so rich we can almost swallow it.
it is the always peering in;
every detail ever mapped by the senses,
alive and singing with inner meaning.
the patterns in the clouds,
painted against the crescendo of the sea,
the thrust of a flower blooming,
courageous from barren earth.
it is hearing every instrument hum
beautiful refrains,
interlaced and layering,
weaving exquisite stories,
in dramatic, swelling landscape;
but never belonging
to the symphony.
we live with the questions
for we can never accept
there is no final answer.

— *Emma Blas*

—Feuillemort—
we were taught to fear
the change,
mourn the fading of life
in the falling leaf;
when it is in the turning
we find the beauty of life.
the sun and moon,
the stars and sky,
the tide and shore,
death and life,
rise and fall,
day to night;
one eternally chasing the other
in the constant
coming and going;
for even something
so grand and yet undefined
as the divine,
found itself sometimes lonely,
bursting to share
in this exquisite ache
of existence.

- Emma Blas

Symphonies of the Wild-Hearted

—Persephone's walk—

can you imagine how the first amber leaf of the year sounds as it kisses the ground? reluctant harbinger, it brings us back around the sun, dragging the earth into winter; when like a klaxon, it summons our sweet persephone homebound.

hades is waiting for her to walk back to him, just beyond the three-jawed cerberus. he is grinning. he and the dog are both grinning.
slack-jawed.

there are too many teeth.

as ears of corn turn golden, crowning harvest wreaths, the birds cease to herald the dawn. she walks backwards.

in the rustle of the leaves, on winter's telling breath, she asks softly of us, that we not forget the pulse of the sun, as it beats on our chest. she walks backwards.

"remember me sweet one, as the warmth heating your blood to passions." she walks backwards.

"remember me my child, as the rumba deep in the belly of the earth." she walks backwards.

"remember me my light, when blackness drops like a curtain." "remember me my love, when you feel the sun has forgotten you, for we will come back around, to touch again." "remember me my songbird, with the wind, mad or mild."

"remember me my little savage, as all things wild."

— Emma Blas

—Expectant—

each year began
the same,
burying
seeds of hope
in expectation.

suffocated,
the year died
before taking a breath.
waiting for eggs to hatch.

fell a tear,
every bitter fear
come true.

swollen with the sorrow
of another year
beached,
no sea to take me.
i cried for the life i never had.

the life i didn't want,
the arms that would never hold me,
the sons i would never sing to
and the daughters i had never lost.

i cried for the mother who had
birthed me full of her dreams.

seven tears fell into the dawn
of this year,
caught by the king of tides.
removing his skin,
under the moon,
he gathered me up,
loving me until i was empty
and full at the same time.

the fullness of the moon remained
long after he had left with the ebb
of the tide for his salty palace.
my waters break the coming of fall.
i harvest you, fruit of my labours,
planting other years with hope.

— *Emma Blas*

Symphonies of the Wild-Hearted

—A moment in time—
wet sand reflects the sky,
be it blue or grey,
clouds billowing
mottle the shoreline
crisscrossed by sandpiper
and seagull feet,
hopping between
hollowed out seashell litter,
feasted upon until discarded.
the sand makes no complaint,
whilst it holds all
these forms and images
for their short legacy of existence,
until it is history,
rewriting itself again.

– Emma Blas

—Price of progress—

the air tasted of dandelions, bright yellow with sunshine and the hope of coming spring. fields sprang soft mattresses under feet, running toward promised dreams. lungs burning and cheeks aglow, eyes bright with youth of what they didn't yet know, they made a pact in spit and blood, sealed under summer's haze and innocence of different days, spent in unashamed, simple ways.

time passed as it is wont to do, can't stand still, without new seconds on the clock, for memories to make and be forgot. the rivers swam began to dry; some families broke, a lover died. farms outgrew their hedgerows, cut away at fallow fields. the next generation kept out of simple pleasures, searched more complex ones, found themselves lost down dark alleys on the wrong side of town; for now there were sides; wrongs and rights, yours and mine.

one night, five brothers again met; separated by time and the marks that spoke whether they were up, or down on their luck. those down felt no joy in the gathering, only lack; those up felt they had something they must protect. with minds locked they cut the bonds of friendship in fear with fists; cut the bonds of yesteryear's blood pacts with suspicion and mistrust. innocence so long lost and in pain, forgot. turning from each other they went their separate ways. the air tasted like regret, black with smog and the creep of coming fall.

the boar fell to leaves
old age and winter's just breath
will pick his bones clean

- *Emma Blas*

Symphonies of the Wild-Hearted

—Eucalyptus tears—
once a year,
she cries
silver ribbons
for home;
her dreams
are pungent,
oiled;
a lick of fire
is all it takes
to be reborn.

— Emma Blas

—Slip and slide—
it slunk into the water
all curves
and oily feathers,
all slip and slide,
glide,
until flap
and wriggle,
a silver fish
is breaking its back
to escape the beak;
until
flipped back,
into gullet,
it is swallowed
whole.
in less than a second,
the cormorant is diving again,
slip, slide and glide.

— Emma Blas

—Savage—

i see a beast
running with the waves,
savage and wild;
a beast wanting
to crush everything in its path,
grind it all into the shore;
a boat into splinters,
shells to dust,
brand the sand
with its mark.

i see that beast
in your eyes,
the hunger, primal,
dilating wide and black;
a moment of madness
only placated
by getting your way.

i see that beast
in the way your tongue
flicks to the corner
of your mouth,
already tasting the fats
marbled in the flesh,
dripping into your mouth.

i see that beast
in your hands,
trembling to grasp
and drag me down,
to tear at the doors i closed,
shutting my soft meat away.

i see that beast
in our teeth,
we all bite,
in some way or another;
though watch the wolves
as they take down their prey,
see how first,
they tear out the throat
so that it doesn't suffer
being eaten alive.

- Emma Blas

Symphonies of the Wild-Hearted

—Next generation—
the claw of a root
hooks into crevice
and grows.
when winter screams
that it has no place here,
grappling from all sides,
the sapling limed
in earth and rock
and scree,
will find other roots
to tangle with
and hold the skirts
of the mountain together,
like a daughter, grown.

— *Emma Blas*

—Why did the blackbirds come to land on the sand?—
i had only ever seen seagulls
and sandpipers alight here;
along with an occasional cormorant
stopping off in winter,
staggering corpulent body,
and broad, broad wing,
inelegant on land;

hawks circle almost without end
overhead,
though never come to land;
so why did the blackbirds come,
to land on the sand?

they were not crows or ravens,
come picking at the bones
of the seagull's corpse,
slowly being hollowed out nearby;
i can find no trace of shell, husk,
nor carcass
in their wake;
only a tiny print,
of tiny feet,
left in the sand;

so why did the blackbirds come
to land on the sand?
was it a game of bravery
to play against the tide,
did they eat a tiny morsel,
or take away something glittering,
left behind by man?

i hear them
in the trees
close by,
now I am here
and they are gone.

- *Emma Blas*

—Honey—

it is winter and the bumble bee
is drunk on the idea of spring;
searching for nectar
in scraggy grass.
an open window,
too much possibility
for a trusting heart
smelling flowers
even in metal and glass.
i carry blossom in my pocket
to feed these sweet souls,
always leaving the door open,
so that they may come and go.

- Emma Blas

—Under the moon—
i have spent so long
haunting shadows,
the devil cut out my tongue.
how now can i howl
to run with brother wolf?
how to ravel this knot
of sparrows pecking
behind these ribbed bars,
when i cannot sing their song?
all that is left,
is to let the fire burn,
for under the moon
we all bloom alone.

- Emma Blas

Symphonies of the Wild-Hearted

—Near blind—
i think of the mole,
   gentle clawed paws
      feeling the reassuring response
         of the earth to her, firm but yielding.
            and I do not want to give

my faith blindly, but
   put it where it also
      puts its belief in me;
         both held and impelled
            into the obsidian tunnel ahead

by trusting that this empty
   space will breach me
      to a freedom, that doesn't
         live in cloud or idea, beyond
            my own sense of wonder.

— Emma Blas

—Come sunshine or rain—

the sun may shine tomorrow,
but equally, it may rain;
no matter how many times
i listen to the weatherman
or how many weathermen and women
tell me about warm fronts
and areas of increasing
or decreasing pressure;
it gives me no more certainty
over the unknown,
than living a healthy and hopeful life
gives me over the day i will die.
one day i will lose my mother,
my father and my brother;
or maybe they will lose me.
we do not know how it will go,
we do not know the year,
the why or the how.
i know that i will cry
and that my loss will be greater
than the trees losing their leaves to winter;
i know that i will stand alone
whilst the trees wrap themselves again in spring;
and that even though my heart will be so heavy
that if i walked into a river, i would drown,
i would never wish to see them fallen,
lain on their sides,
turning back alone to the earth.
so it is that i am here,
standing with umbrella,
that may also provide shade;
as the rain falls on my face,
and the sun shines in my eyes,
i am drenched, bright to rainbow,
tongue stuck out to drink up
little sips of love;
and i vow as i bow
nose to these roots,
to enjoy
how the rich black dirt
that clings to them,
is fat with the juice of life.

- Emma Blas

—Below the horizon—
i need not scales nor gills
to appreciate the wonder
under this world;
i long to peel off
neoprene,
take too this skin,
and sink deeper;
to be neither fish,
mammal,
or even woman;
yet still to belong
to this current of life
beneath the surface.
let me slip
below the horizon,
into the big blue
reflected
by my wanting eyes.

— Emma Blair

—Incorporated—
i have taken to believing
the birds are singing me
into being;
every trill fills
and firms
out the flesh, incorporating,
this incorporeal thing,
into a woman;
woven of twigs,
leaves
and lost feathers.
when their song is finished,
i will fly;
taking the earth with me,
to join with the sky
in a full embrace.

- Emma Blas

—Dandelion clocks—
intoxicated by spring,
i sit in the meadow
in a drunk stupor;
sun shifts through trees,
a flickering haze
as dandelion cotton and pollen
mingle on the breeze;
tiny wrens almost deafen,
exploding into ear splitting trills.
i watch the butterflies
dance across the daisies,
tasting with their feet;
and wish i could taste with mine;
barefoot sipping on clover like wine,
drinking up buttercups
grandaddy used to twirl
under my chin,
making my neck shine.
instead i taste nothing,
but a thirst,
to drown in the dew
and undo time.

— Emma Blas

—Quiet—
the clover has crawled
over the lawn of my body,
i am watching bees
drink deep of fragrant nectar;

if i keep lying here
the ants will build colonies,
nested under my skin,
worms will burrow,

the earth will breathe,
but i will be filled with holes;
when the voles come
i will be too cavernous,

to be a person anymore,
but there will be beauty.
if i disturb the butterflies
opening their wings,

uproot the strawberries
starting to pucker into fruit,
there will be emptiness,
bare soil, a gaping, ugly hole.

— Emma Blas

Symphonies of the Wild-Hearted

—The blooming—
the flowers bleed,
it is part of the blooming.
even buds so fresh
they know not a word of
the bloody path
in the world ahead;
as inevitable as the seed
caught flying on the wind,
or carried on the body
of a small creature,
so too the bleeding.
red roses, white lilies,
yellow dahlias, purple iris,
pink hibiscus, lavender and lilacs;
they all bleed
as they open to fertility,
whether choosing to open
or pass their blood
to the next generation,
or not.
a choice,
not an expectation,
theirs to make alone.
if the bleeding is as inevitable
as a woman's tears,
why not help her stem
the flow?

— *Emma Blas*

—Human-beings—
i watch this tiny ball
of fur and bone
and teeth and claw;
its instinct to hunt,
to chase and catch,
driving it to its nature
before it has left my walls
or had to hunt a meal;
i wonder that maybe
we aren't just made
to run and cry and fight
and fuck after all.
we dress it up,
a search for meaning
beyond our borders,
to find the truth
in rubbing them out;
but maybe we are just beasts
heeding the call of the wild.

- *Emma Blas*

Symphonies of the Wild-Hearted

—He says he wants to fuck me—
my legs are wide open,
for the fabric of existence
to be penetrated;
but i don't believe
a job so big,
could be done by a man.
he says he wants to fuck me,
but it seems so binary,
just ones and zeros;
micro,
fleeting,
when the universe
is so vast,
and i can be fucked
by all that is,
all at once.

he says he wants to fuck me,
but i want a lover
to dissolve me;
water to my salt,
fire to my air,
turning leaf to soil,
nature claiming me
back to her embrace.

if i want to be fucked,
it is by her;
and i do want
to have her
fuck my brains out,
or rather off;
senses filled until i burst,
a white dwarf,
post super nova,
spent,
returned to the galactic scrap heap,
undone.

so, it is done,
she has bitten off my head,
i am, or was,
her praying mantis mate,
made obsolete
in my search for wisdom,
headless, i watch in peace.

– *Emma Blas*

—Wild rose—

i see your limbs climbing,
so gangly and fluid,
to tangle, sky bound,
in your hair, as sun bleached
it tumbles into your freckles;
and even i long to brush
lips across your shoulder
when it slips, free,
in your reaching,

                    thorn less,
                    for the stars;

just for a moment,
just to taste freedom again,

                    just a sip;

before the rose,

                    [an obstruction
                    or distraction,
                    too wild,
                    uncontrollable,
                    too alive]

is cut back;
all its wildness contained;
until the next spring stirs
in her loins,
and she knows again
the possibility of living

                    unbound.

- Emma Blas

Symphonies of the Wild-Hearted

―Embodied―

walking this tapestry of memory
through all her seasons,
twists and turns of weather,
capricious day to night;
has taught me how to love.

eyes trace the landscape tenderly,
stroke familiar curves,
delight in the sight of new shoots
nestling into their lullabies.

i know the blooms that follow
will fall to brown at the call of winter,
but it does not feel a lie;

she sighs my name like a lover,
as she is whispering 'home',
we are caught in the intense embrace
of those who know saying goodbye
is as inevitable as breathing.

i choose not to weep
over the red flowers,
petals scattered on the wind,
they are as much me now
as the air in my lungs,
and the soil under
the soles of my feet.
even the darkest clouds
are edged in light.

― Emma Blas

—Hold me—
we wait for night to fall
but it is the day that fades away,
exiting in peaches and pinks,
a parting gift to gently soothe us
into grey before we thicken
like the night, sink to sleep;
what first thought a curtain,
drops to blanket, swaddled comfort
for our daily ritual of letting go.
the longer the shadow
the more ardent the embrace.

- *Emma Blas*

—Human worship—

i have no trouble
loving feathered, furry or green
things; even if i don't know how
to call it by a name,
i can love it just for being
part of this world;
but make it of metal
or give it skin,
call it man,
then i will worship
until my prayers
go unanswered,
and wonder why flesh
cannot perform miracles;
why it cannot be more than
ephemeral, a being,
living human,
filled to the brim
with the unknown,
trying just to hold on
to a moment,
any moment,
in the constant fear
of the endless drop below.

we want to make this fraction
of the universe's breath feel real,
to be more than the blink of an eye;
so we ask each other be gods,
notch time on our belts
and bed posts;
pray to flesh
that will wither and rot,
to an idea that will decay,
someday;
carve sculptures that stay,
but are no more real
than their likeness, just
as cold to the touch;
sinners can be saints
and fools heroes,
but balanced on a pedestal,
somebody has to fall.

we were supposed to follow
the weather, stepping in time
with the seasons,
rouse ourselves with the day
and fall into sleep
with the sink of night;
we were born to swim
with the river
in ebb and flow,
not push back the tide;
we were meant to follow
the sun, chase the moon,
store the harvest
and save the seeds for spring;

we were meant to offer thanks,
to the earth for every meal,
we gobble down;
we were meant to protect
the beings; we,
being this, one, among
ten million, others,
sharing
in guardianship
the forests,
the water, the air,
our earth;

we were meant to care
for each other,
to hold each other
when nightmares bleed into day,
take each other by the hand
when we have lost our way;
but we were never,
ever,
meant to follow,
blindly,
in faith,
or reason,
man.

— Emma Blas

Symphonies of the Wild-Hearted

—Prickly pear—
juice runs hot pink
down your
c h i n.
i reach it
just before the back
of your absentminded
h a n d,
kiss it from your
f a c e.
you turn, e y e s
smile, - gleam, corners crinkle
the sweet peace of one
who has found their place
in the world,
as loved.
i continue putting
the bandaid on your
f i n g e r.
sat shaded by the nopal,
happily in your
s h a d o w,
escaping old father
              time.

— Emma Blas

―The weight of existence―

how can we measure
this weight of existence?
surely not in pounds
or ounces,
by dollars,
or the number
of syllables
uttered by a mouth in a day?

the depth of a footprint
left in the sand
cannot tell the size of a heart
of a person,
any more than know
the number of grains
clasped, or foresee
when they will fall
from a hand.

― Emma Blas

Lucia Haase

@writer_in_residence

Lucia Haase has been writing poetry for 20 years as the direct result of a spiritual experience which had occured in her life. She has won numerous awards for her poems and has had music composed to one of her poems. Most of what she writes is in formal verse, with nature or human emotion themes, but there is an occasional free verse poem written also. Her favorite form to write in is the sonnets. She is inspired by many of the famous poets, such as William Wordsworth, Robert Frost and Edwin Arlington Robinson.

—Lulled—

Sun drenched sails capture flow
when the tide moves high or low;
calming to my soul, I owe

quiet, even keel time
winded at the helm where I'm
finding deeper peace for me...

— Lucia Haase

—Seaside—

I write
from the sea, moving my sail
to the wind's direction-
to the waves cadence.

I find
in the depths that come before me
and rise within me,
some cloud reflection.

My heart
is a shell, one of multitudes,
tossing and turning to shore
until someone picks it up
and listens to the ocean's roar.

— Lucia Haase

−The key−

Winding ivy silently clinging, lilting
captures quiet essences I have longed for.
Soothing breezes call to me near a doorway
offering a solace.

Latches creak while opening up the door here;
garden flowers wait for my presence, singing.
Scents and colors beautifully beg my eyesite,
glistening star-like.

Sparrows flitting joyously chirp and linger;
pillowed paths lie beckoning strides of senses.
Secret places blooming inside withhold the
key to my heartstrings.

—Refuge—

There's a country in the barn
that cannot be seen outside-
that is different than the land's
hailing deeper, vast and wide.

There's a quiet resonating
through the weathered boards, that's good,
and a place to call my own-
had I too been made of wood.

— Lucia Haase

—Celebration—

In the flowering,
let it be panoramic-
at least, on this day

as the sun drenched
waves rolling in
have their say...

where a hand held
warmth heralds peace
next to none

from the shoal
to the strand of
a party of one.

— Lucia Haase

—Tapestry—
Here in the weave
a peaceful scene,
nature woven-
Water serene...

a bridge connected,
a home residing
and onto this paper-
the swans gliding.

— Lucia Haase

—Haiku—
under the ginkgo,
cooled by multitudes of fans
in hands of the wind

— Lucia Haase

—Momentum—
Here on the cliff,
time is a train
beneath my feet-
tread I've to gain...

and looking in
over the ocean,
movement of depth
captures emotion

towards the horizon,
clouds almost fleeting...
cry of the seagulls-
wind on my being.

— Lucia Haase

—Landscape artist—
Discovering a palette
for the sky-
a brush forward,
a blending spree...

experimenting
with colors-
choosing what's
complimentary,

and as time
become spent
without constraint-

finding you've
chosen the
right paint.

— Lucia Haase

―Chocolate and roses―
A truffle here, a nougat there,
the chocolate light and dark;
unopened candy everywhere-
each piece an inner spark.

A bouquet here, a nosegay there-
the budding of the stems,
and roses, roses everywhere
the vast horizon hems.

— Lucia Haase

―Butterfly―
If you flutter up
and you set your sight,
there's a victor's cup
where the blooms grow bright...

when a call to wings
on a journey planned
leaves you fluttering,
even when you land.

— Lucia Haase

—The crocus—
Now breathes the dawning crocus, like the day-
a burst of verse from flame to fervent fire.
Now from the grounded depths of muses way
springs forth a song as boldly as a choir.
In breezes found, here blossoms inspired words-
bright petals sought to savor, one by one
within the soil where thawing has begun;
the crocus thrives...and have you heard the birds?

— Lucia Haase

—In the woodland—
'Neath the heart
that's the bridge,
flows a vein
to the ridge-
water's course
through the soil
here amidst
weather's toil;
where I stand,
beats my heart-
water's course,
spirit's chart...
flowing stream
to the Ridge
pulsing on
'neath the bridge..

— Lucia Haase

Symphonies of the Wild-Hearted

—A field of tulips—

Find me a field of tulips
bathed in quiet, yellow spirit;
lead me into the silence to rejoice
and let me hear it.

Find me in the field,
although I know I am just one
like each bloom before me
with each day begun.

— Lucia Haase

—Catch me now—

Catch me now
while I'm falling
for the leaves-
Autumn's calling;
Just as they,
falling free-
freefalling
just like me...
Hill to knoll
far and wide,
I shall take them
all inside...
captive by
the heartland's brow-
in the falling,
catch me now.

— Lucia Haase

—Winter forest—
Let me
bare like the wood
I see

my soul,
in a cold world
from knoll

to clime,
beautifully warm
in rhyme.

- *Lucia Haase*

—I love a lake—
I love a lake at any time
in any season's chosen rhyme
like any poem's metered chime
reflecting peace,
to wade into the deep to mime
my heart's increase.

Of waves that rise and dip to shore,
like flow of ink then more and more-
the wind goes knocking on my door...
a dream awake
that moves my spirit to the core-
I love a lake.

- *Lucia Haase*

Symphonies of the Wild-Hearted

―Salt and clouds―
Realities come forth like rain
upon a stark and weathered dock.
His sunken dreams lie far away
within the currents fateful clock.
He sailed far out to open sea
equipped with loves demanding ship,
yet couldn't see the tidal waves
or how a heavy anchor slips.

― Lucia Haase

―Shapes of clouds―
Shapes of clouds,
kinds of days
meeting up-
parting ways...

air-bound sighs,
moving on
seconds, hours
minutes gone...

skies of gray
or of blue,
sun or rain
in the hue;

days ahead
floating by-
shapes of clouds
in the sky.

― Lucia Haase

—Sonnet—

That rippling traveler water, passes by
and leaves beyond the bridge her lovely scroll
to touch on lilypads beneath that lie
upon reflective paintings of my soul.
Thus, fragrance stirs surrounding me this day;
I see the lilies like I always do.
Each bloom becomes to me a seeming play
grown in the fragrance and the breath of you.
You in each blossom of my way of fearing-
the words I meant to say and could not tell;
you in soft movement, you within my hearing-
my walking on the bridge, a lonely bell,
and through the reeds, your voice- swelling, thinning
lost in the rippling pond and wind's beginning.

— Lucia Haase

Symphonies of the Wild-Hearted

—Into the wood—
Into the wood, some roses fade
into the grain of memories made
as others linger, standing out;
often they are spoken about and reconveyed.

Held in the structure and the weave,
the roses fade but never leave;
remembrance flares from time to time
into the deeper wood where rhyme, the heart retrieves.

— Lucia Haase

—My Heart, Your Heart—
My heart, your heart and the world's-
seed to root to thriving tree,
side by side, as meant to be-
my heart, your heart and the world's...
peace abounding, love unfurled
in the forest...don't you see?
My heart, your heart and the world's-
seed to root to thriving tree.

— Lucia Haase

―Villanelle: the meadow's ways―
There's always those seasons with the Meadow's ways
with a winded scattering of seeds to and fro,
from the ground swell up to the nurturing gaze

of the sunlight's warmth through the gentle haze.
All the seeds we spread-where do they go?
There's always those seasons with the Meadow's ways;

for the constant growth is a sure fire praise-
in the root of the heartland, let it show
from the ground swell up to the nurturing gaze

of the falling rain or the sunlight's rays
where the florets rise and the seedlings blow-
there's always those seasons with the meadow's ways.

Make each month a season in the maze
for the seeds to kindle, soon to show
from the ground swell up to the nurturing gaze...

In the freeing breeze, in your numbered days-
for our earthly time is short, you know...
there's always those season with the Meadow's ways
from the ground swell up to His nurturing gaze.

― Lucia Haase

Symphonies of the Wild-Hearted

Jessica Walsh

@her__odyssey

Jessica grew up in southern Louisiana, between the Cypress trees and the Spanish Moss. She was an avid reader at a very young age and began writing in her early teens. Her adventurous spirit took her cross country to the Pacific Northwest where she resided in Seattle and surrounding areas for several years before making Louisiana her home once again. A passion for animals and the outdoors, obsessions with coffee and music, her spirituality, and an unequivocal bond with her eight year old daughter all fuel her everyday life. Having personal experiences with both, Jessica speaks and writes often on the topics of child abuse and addiction recovery.

—Skin deep—

Someone saw worth in my beauty,
Now, I am chained,
Andromeda enslaved again,
But this time no god will save me.
I shall wither on this rock,
Just to please an eye,
Though I'd rather please an ear,
Or invoke a tear,
With my soulful melodies.
Perhaps my voice will carry,
Satisfy a soul in peril,
Before I waste away under the sea.
For that, I sing to thee.

- Jessica Walsh

—Deluge—

The culprit
One rogue idea
That strays from my head
Into my chest
The starting
Of a perfect storm
And I have no shelter
For this kind of chaos

- Jessica Walsh

Symphonies of the Wild-Hearted

—The gambler—
High stakes
Whiskey coated air
Smoke scented perfume
A game of chance
I was all in
Unclothed, unearthed
You folded before the river came
What a pity
The hand was yours to win
You caved before the final sin
Either you called my bluff
Or wanted a way out
I rake my winnings
As I button my blouse
Watching, as you leave me
With nothing but broken hearts

— *Jessica Walsh*

—Serenity in memory—

I tried to find your memory
But like ripples in a tide pool
   when small stones are thrown,
Or when tiny little fish come to the surface,
   searching for bits of nothing —
The reflection is muddled
And only stillness will do, to bring back
   the image of you
Stillness is hard to find, in the mirror
   of my panic-stricken mind
Frantic to find what we once were
I reach between the folds of drowning sheets
Where our kindred souls used to meet
Where eyes would swim in ecstasy and
   minds meld on parallel planes
A place for hearts to go insane —
Were we those little fish, or were we destined
   to feast on bigger things?
Hungry for each other without the curse of tattered heartstrings?
Only questions remain, and I am left
   digging in the mud of mire,
   begging for enough water to serve as glass
Stillness, I seek
Without clarity, I am meek
For your memory, I yearn
Be calm little tide pool, so I might see the reflection
   of what I once knew
So I can learn to live a life without you

— Jessica Walsh

—Scavenger hunt—

Stranded, along a forgotten road,
I work fervently to find a way home,
To the motherly arms of a warm page,
Full of poems wrinkled with age.

Stooping, scouring, against the clock,
Sacrificing skin to unmovable rocks,
Uncovering words laden with tears,
Layers of grief that outlived the years.

Deep, dark secrets showing me the way,
Sadness as my compass, art as my slave,
Digging for truth, for gut wrenching pain,
Make it sound lovely, they said...
And a poet you shall remain.

— Jessica Walsh

—Battle wounds—

There is a hitch in my step
Look carefully and you might notice
   a limp
A stagger
A souvenir of war
Embedded shrapnel in my thigh
I escaped death
Only because you had bad aim
   after you pulled the pin
Nonetheless, there is still the memory
   trapped beneath my skin
A victim, I am not
A war, I have fought
And I kiss my legs each night
With the intensity of a soldier
   and the passion of a poet

— *Jessica Walsh*

—Familiar—

I knew you once,
Nestled in the arms of stars,
Bathing in the light
Of an awestruck moon.

You had been asleep,
For lifetimes,
Dreaming the same old dream,
A lover's tale on repeat.

Thousands of pennies,
And countless birthday candles,
What hard work this wishing is,
To hunt the elusive shooting star.

All the while, I was there,
Touching your cheek,
Singing lullabies,
Enticing your eyes to see.

— *Jessica Walsh*

Symphonies of the Wild-Hearted

—Barefoot and bereft—
There is no taking back
What I have already given,
No time to waste between sheets,
Or stall on the road I have driven.

I search for you off the beaten path,
Play hide and seek with my love's ideal,
I search in dead woods and dry ponds,
In empty spaces, expecting to feel.

Perhaps I need a new map,
Drawn with wisdom rather than pain,
Become a scholar of real love,
Before I dare look for you again.

— Jessica Walsh

—Ambiguous—
Silence is both my enemy
and my enlightenment.
It is both the hour of fear
when the demons
have their way,
and the hour
in which I pray.

— Jessica Walsh

— When he is the dusk —
The day skipped its twilight hours
Jumping from cloudy and gray
To honest and black
No relief from overpacked roads
Full of battling headlight glares
No pining at dusk
Lonely windows full of vacant stares
No transition from charade to chagrin
Straight to the barest of bones
Exposing the heat of frigid lips
The punch in the gut return
To the terror of being alone
Soon, it will be time to dream
Of green, of skin, of calmer seas
Of a day not afraid of eve
Of sunset escapes from reality

- Jessica Walsh

Symphonies of the Wild-Hearted

—Chaos as an Overture—

Air speeds through my lungs
   like wind chimes
My song reliant on the breeze
I pray for gust, for gale —
   the ability to exhale
I am just an instrument
   begging for a storm
Silence in the sun
   does not suit me
In the raging wind —
   I have found my home

— *Jessica Walsh*

—Choreography—

To err —
   to tread too loudly on glass
To fall into arms of second chance
Is the gift of bruising
Adjust your legs —
   rearrange the pattern
   in which your feet kiss the ground
Change your shoes
Reinvent your self instruction
Ask not the glass
   to morph to metal
But, listen to your music
   and dance differently

— *Jessica Walsh*

— Gypsies —

Do not mock
the stargazers.
They are the wishers,
the dreamers,
the firework seekers —
the lovers
of all things magical
and worshippers
of the wild.

— Jessica Walsh

— Serenade —

Sweet crescent song
I hear you through the branches
And the hum of the curious owl
Harmonies that touch my hem
That reach under my skirt
And climb up to kiss my eyelids
Seductive melody
Under watchful gaze of sky
Touch me again
Where I need to feel the most
Pluck my heartstrings
Banish my ghosts
Sweet crescent song
Lull me to dream under lamplight
While your soulful echoes
Chant his name
Sweet muse of moon
Make me a believer again

— Jessica Walsh

Symphonies of the Wild-Hearted

—Faith in skin and voice—
Solace is the night that guides me
Comfort in the arms that hold
Tempered are the thoughts that find me
Patient as the truth unfolds
Wayfaring heart reflects a hazel moon
Just before the dawn
Luminous hair of a golden hue
Nestled in my arms
A voice like husk and dirt and poems
Ripples through the air
A hush like need and heat and bone
Dared to strip me bare
An undertow of glistening dreams
Pulls me to the edge
From charming, chiseled, dampened lips
Let the truth be said

— Jessica Walsh

—Trepidation—

I find myself here, yet again.
Stopped at the crossroads
   of run away or dive in —
my ankles already damp,
my eyes already swimming
   in a shade of lake (the hue of water
   reflecting pines),
my nervous fingers groping for a sign.
I have been drawn to green
   so many times,
and each has left me dry.
And I wonder, as I
   brave the incoming tide —
Will this be the one to drown me?

— Jessica Walsh

—Tangled—

I have dreamed
of all the ways
I could be set free.
Rescued from the whipping post.
I am untethered.
Unraveled.
Completely undone.
And yet, I have never
felt so entwined.
Beautiful what a heart can do,
should it be so inclined.

— Jessica Walsh

—Tenacity in spring—
Birdsong breaks through the gray,
like sadness giving way to bloom —
and I, the weed,
my roots dancing their way
through thoughts of you —
my petals soaking in hints of sun;
and I am burning into wildflower.

— *Jessica Walsh*

—Tenacious—

Love me
The way a lion rips at flesh
Ferociously
With the unfaltering will
To stay alive
Love me like that

— *Jessica Walsh*

—Resuscitation—

Hold my pain for a moment
Flexible, pliable pain
Hold it delicately, by the stem
Let it wilt
But let it not
Lose the beauty within
Hold the horizon for a moment
Glorious, golden dream
Hold it firmly, by the seams
Let it shine
But let it not
Overshadow the moon
Hold my air for a moment
When it is thick with humid rain
Breathe for me
Make it all beautiful again

— Jessica Walsh

―Ode to the two―

Last night, such a lovely dream,
Sailing wild on the open seas,
With two men, of the same name,
One with a grin, the other with a pen.

One danced, uncaged and free,
His gypsy spirit calling to me,
Bass and drums and tambourines,
We twirled and whirled unabashedly.

Oh, how his antics made me smile,
Putting my shyness to bed for a while,
Endless talk and nonsensical rhymes,
Floating on laughter all through the night.

Then the other, with the same name,
Sitting quietly, chewing on his pen,
Gazing at stars, romancing the sky,
Sonnets and song carved in his mind.

A beauty he was, cast in bronze,
With sultry eyes and a foreign tongue,
A poetic angel with a hint of sin,
Taking me to places I have never been.

He drew my smile with a different style,
With curvy lips that traveled for miles,
Full of charm and mystery,
Speaking huskily to the lover in me.

Two men, of the exact same name,
One a friend, the other a dream,
One with happy kisses to my cheek,
The other can make a blind heart see.

Two muses to my eager pen,
Where fear ended and courage began,
Turning madness into a fountain of words,
Now I am seen, now I can be heard.

— Jessica Walsh

Symphonies of the Wild-Hearted

—Hunger—

I crave a fantastical love
The way a shadow craves water
Or autumn covered sidewalks
   long for a spring breeze
It is the relief, the release that I seek
Like rolling waves breaking the calm of the sea
Give to my ears, this music that I need
A resonance of beats at perfect speed
A harmony of hard and soft
Of this I speak, of this I want
Like a pen craves a muse
What I need is you

— *Jessica Walsh*

—Souvenir—

I wish I could bottle
the green of your eyes,
for days when the
barren, brown landscape
has me longing
for a touch of spring.

— *Jessica Walsh*

—Confession—
Tell her
She is beautiful
How she flows
Like ink
From an eager hand
Like a river
Carving barren land

— Jessica Walsh

—Satin in the form of poetry—
His words, like cotton
Offer reprieve from silence
Soft and ink soaked
Slide slowly up my skin
Like poetry
Ramblings of a romantic
With a love story to tell
Over my knees
And up my thighs
These words, they gather
And settle
In the fire of my eyes

— Jessica Walsh

—Owner's manual—
My heart is a template
Instructions for loving me
scribed in stone
And he reads me —
like a book
Turning words to clay
Watering
the roadmap to my soul
On wobbly legs, I walk
In gentle hands, I cave
Under moon
he studies
Under stardust
I let him learn
In surrender, I burn

- Jessica Walsh

―First kiss―
Take me back
To the second
The earth shifted
And my head tilted
And hands sprouted
From the dirt
To wrap around my ankles
To keep me firmly rooted
In that very moment
The most amazing now
I have ever breathed
The taste on my lips
The turn of your head
As you whispered "fireworks"
And we watched the blaze of sky
With stardust
Burning in our eyes

- *Jessica Walsh*

Symphonies of the Wild-Hearted

—For Sarah—

I would give you
the moon ...
if I could.
This lifetime,
and everyone to come.
A bouquet of moons.
Yes, that just might do.
Anything else
would pale
in comparison to you.

— Jessica Walsh

—Sun god—

Dapper, is he
Who stands tall
   among the reeds
Out-twirling the cattails
And dancing in the breeze
The one who makes the wind blush
When the clouds insist on gray
Soft hands with a Midas touch
Shaping sun from a rainy day
Dapper, is he
Not in the beauty of his face
But, how he makes room for love
When the world
   runs out of space

— Jessica Walsh

—Unspoken—

Only he,
can look into my eyes
and make it sound
like a promise.
Only I,
can stare back
and make it sound
like poetry.

— Jessica Walsh

Wildflower

@wildflower.musings

Wildflower is a Biology graduate turned newly poet, writer, and now author. Always having been a lover of reading poetry and dabbling with writing it, she didn't start seriously writing poetry until the start of 2017 through a journey of breaking and healing. Such journeys of love, heartbreak, questioning, healing, and self-discovery can be seen reflected in her work. When she isn't spending her time scribbling in journals, she is spending her time in nature, learning about wildlife, cuddling her cats, capturing moments and details with her camera, picking wildflowers, and questioning the secrets of the universe while never forgetting all its magic.

Symphonies of the Wild-Hearted

—Astral daydreams—
Daydreams of forest trees
and rolling mountains deep.
Daydreams of us tucked away
in secrets of evergreen,
our souls raised above
in flittering dimensions unseen.

— *Wildflower*

—Raging thunderstorm—
Remember those old summer days
when it would pour of rain and we'd
dance in it like children—laughing,
twirling, kissing the wet from each
other's lips and each other's bodies—
not a single care that we were soaked?
That's how we loved, you and I—like
the rain—full of force and all at once,
passion mixed with lightning with each
thunder beat of our hearts. We were not
a light spring sun shower, we were a
raging thunderstorm, beckoning the
darkening sky and each other's hands.

— *Wildflower*

―Golden touch―
The morning wakes me as the sun pours gold
through the window and blankets the edges
of earth and my skin just the same.
The heat of the sun gives me chills and it
so often resembles how the warmth
of your hands do the same.
Oh, how I long for you to touch me
the way the sun touches everything
with gold as it rises.

- Wildflower

―Autumn Goodbyes―
Crisp air and fallen leaves
carrying whispered goodbyes.
They, too, must leave
the very thing they spent
so long holding on to.

- Wildflower

Symphonies of the Wild-Hearted

—Parachute dreams—
We found our love
living in dandelion dreams—
abundant, yet fleeting—
gone with the wind
in parachute wishes.

— *Wildflower*

—Frostbite—
Goodbye is a whispered word
I never wanted between us,
but like winter, it finds its way
into our frigid bones, aching
with the frostbite of a love gone cold.

— *Wildflower*

—Fractured ice—
Cracked ice so perfectly matches
the fractures creating art in my heart
from where your hands used to be.
I wonder if I'll make it through
this season of dismal dark.
Will my heart thaw with the ache
to be alive and thrive
like the sleeping earth underneath?

— *Wildflower*

—Hues of you—

The cardinal perched on red oak branch as the hummingbird drinks from the full bellies of hibiscus, and us, splayed on blankets of grass with tangled limbs and arms wrapped. Flushed cheeks from the heat of the sunflower sun and our cherry lips pressed into a kiss, stained from too much red Kool-Aid because all we wanted was to act like kids. *Everything was red.* We watched the sun sink into the earth as watercolor red and orange hues melted into the sky and I couldn't help but think this is what love looks like—what our love looks like: an explosion of fire and souls melting into one another. I'll never forget your maroon shirt, how it was slightly damp with sweat on your chest and I'll never forget how I buried my face in it to hide my pink blushing cheeks when you told me you wanted this forever. I swear the blood in my heart pumped so powerfully that my heart skipped a beat.

Everything was red.

The wind howls as it blows the last of the red oak leaves off the tree, leaving it skeletal and bare. Through the thick fog, I can barely see a blue-grey sky that is hiding a sun underneath; somewhere, but I can't find it—the same way I can't find your hands laced with mine or your warm breath against my neck and all I ever thought we had was time, but now all I can think is how cold my hands are, blue like the shadows in winter—absent of sun, absent of you. *Everything is blue.* I fidget with the bluebird necklace you bought me, telling me it held a promise and I wonder why it let go of that promise; why you let go. And I'll never forget your blue eyes and the way they looked into mine, deep as an ocean as you told me goodbye and I'll never forget your indigo shirt and the way I buried my face in it to comfort my rainfall eyes. I breathe in ice cold air and needle pain forms in my chest and it so perfectly resembles the pain stabbed in my chest from the day you left.

Everything is blue.

— Wildflower

—Nocturnal—

Bats awake from overturned slumber,
wolves howl at the moon,
and owls screech in the black of night.
Isn't it funny how we all cry out
once the sun is swallowed
by the horizon and only the
moon is our witness?
Even I cry out to her, like she
is the only one willing to listen to my darkness
because this is where darkness—the nocturnal—
comes alive.
This is when we learn survival
as we stitch our darkness into strength,
join hands with the night,
and keep our bones sturdy enough to
rise with sun the next day—
even when our lungs are thick
with morning fog.

— Wildflower

—Embers—
This fire within only burns
because of survival;
strength cloaked
in embers.

— Wildflower

—Little bird—
Most days,
I just want to feel
what it feels like
to not have two feet planted
on the ground, but instead
wings through the air,
a swift glide forward,
defying gravity,
defying all that weighs
me down.

— Wildflower

—Conversations with Gaia—

"patience," She whispered to me.

"You are becoming

and becoming takes time.

The butterfly does not rush

the delicate formation

of its wings,

but it will fly.

Patience, my dear.

You will fly."

— *Wildflower*

—Howl—
The wild in me sees
the wild in you.
No, I am not afraid of you.
You and I,
we both know a thing or two
about the moon,
and the wolves, well they
know how to howl our names.

— Wildflower

—Light wanderer—
Not all answers are found, just like
not all fallen trees are heard in a forest,
but it never means they aren't there.
It is okay to take a leap into the unknown;
shooting stars do it every night
and look at how beautifully they shine.
And if you ever lose your way,
look to the epiphytes that cling to tree bark
and how they are always reaching up.
Look up, dear wanderer, and know
the same light you see is the same light
within you. It has always been.
You just have to reach for it. Claim it,
like the stars and moon claim the night
and the thunder claims the beckoning sky.

— Wildflower

—Doubt turned hope—

Doubt is mud slung onto your face
and soaked clothes from a car too close in the rain.
My eyesight is blurred and clothes hang heavy
and each step feels weighted,
like roots holding me in soggy soil,
but isn't life what we make of it?
I am reminded that
wilting isn't always permanent
and the air can steal this weighted wet.
I wipe the mud from my eyes
and the sun is hope seeping into my marrow
and licking the dampness from my skin.
My eyes veer upward and I am reminded of my worth,
because when have you ever seen a sodden bird
unsure that it can still fly?

— *Wildflower*

―Reaching for warmth―
I stretch my arms out
like tree branches,
hoping I can touch the sky;
hoping the sun
can save me
from the coldness
of today.

− Wildflower

―Canyons―
My eyes are as wide as canyons
and moonlight flows in my veins,
for I have never been one to
shy away from curiosity of the unknown.
They have always called me a dreamer—a nine
lives curious cat, a little bird with wings spread;
heart open with an inquisitive mind,
always ready to step into the night
and never afraid to love with my heart
wide open.

− Wildflower

Symphonies of the Wild-Hearted

—Kudzu—
I will not hold this negative
energy inside my chest.
This ribcage is not for
invasive vines to grow
and suffocate me;
it is for sunlight to reach
and flowers to bloom.

— Wildflower

—Petals of snow—
White petals fall delicately from the
pear tree outside the window,
littering the soil with
the softest white, like snow.
My feet no longer
bruised and scratched
from sticks and stones;
they now tread gently
across the smooth velvet earth.
This shedding of hurt
and sorrow has allowed
my scars to heal over,
as the softest whispers of worth
blanket the earth like snow,

like soft white petals.

— Wildflower

—Blooming—
Spring is on the horizon
and I can smell fresh beginnings
and flowers in the air.
The blooming of tulips, daisies, and love.
What will become of this earth
as it explodes into a lush paradise
of color and second chances?
What will become of us
and the gardens of love I wish to grow
in each other's heart?

— Wildflower

—I hope love grows between us—
I will wait here patiently,
letting the rain water your love
drop
by
drop
and letting your love grow
inch by i n c h
for flowers of love take time to bloom.
I am a gardener and admirer,
and I will give you time to grow
all the parts of your love
as I wait here patiently for you.

— Wildflower

Symphonies of the Wild-Hearted

—Gathering the universe—
My love,
I will gather all the stars,
lasso the sun and moon,
and aim all the shooting stars your way
so that you may never be without
warmth, light, and well wishes,
even through the darkest
and coldest of days.

— *Wildflower*

—Tangled limbs—
These tangled tree branches
resemble our tangled limbs
as you lie here in the grass with me,
both looking to the sky
dreaming of faraway places
and what the sunset must look like there,
but wanting to be nowhere else
but here.

— *Wildflower*

—Hopeless romantic—
I tend to fall in love easily;
like with the way a *butterfly flutters by*
or the way birds sing love songs to the sky;
like with the way the sky becomes a canvas each night,
filled with hues of color and then glittering balls of light;
like with the way the good morning sun warms my face
or with the ridges of the whispering trees I so love to trace;
like with the way the mountains look off in the distance
or the way animals survive and flowers bloom with such persistence.

You see, I fall in love easily with many things,
but not quite like the way
I have so easily fallen in love with you.

— *Wildflower*

—Untamed—
Lover, come here,
let me teach you
the way of the wild;
how these hands can be
more primal than delicate,
and these lips,
more untamed than pure.

Lover, push me
into the soil;
I want to be reborn.

— *Wildflower*

—Cherry blossoms—

I want to fall in love with you

the way cherry blossom trees bloom:
> *abundantly, breathtakingly,*
> *and without pause.*

— Wildflower

—Soft landing—
I am an autumn leaf,
a maple samara seed,
a dandelion wish,
a young bluebird fledgling;
all letting go,
holding on to grace,
and hoping for a
soft place to land.

— Wildflower

— Lilac Flowers —

Have you ever been lucky enough
to smell the sweet scent of lilac flowers?
It reminds me how lucky I am
to be loved by you
and how sweet you are
when I breathe you in.
You are like lilac flowers
and I know because of this
I will never tire of you.
I will press you into these pages
and in the spaces between my fingers.
I will allow you to grow in all the
spaces I have for you,
closest to the window of my heart
so that each night I can fall asleep
and each morning I can wake
to the smell of lilac flowers—
to the sweet scent of you.

— Wildflower

Symphonies of the Wild-Hearted

—Gaia—

I press my feet to the ground and dig my fingers into the soft rich soil—damp and cool against my skin. I breathe in the fresh air as I shut my eyes. I hear the music of nature fill my ears—the rustle of leaves, the melodies of birds, the gentle mountain breeze—as a smile starts to tug at the edges of my lips. My spine meets Earth as I lie back—letting Her hold me like She always has. Every inch of my body, bare skinned and glowing in the sun, connects to the ground or to the air—all of Her offerings engulf me. Her and I are one. I got lost somewhere along the way; my path littered with too much and my eyes and feet finding nothing but darkness and wandering, always wandering. Searching for a path, a light, a hand. It can be easy to get lost in darkness when you don't know where to look and sometimes, we lose pieces of ourselves amongst the destruction. Though the Earth, if you pause for a moment, will gently guide your feet to ground and eyes to light. She will remind you that if you can't find a home in others, you have a home within yourself, a home within this Earth, and a home within the cosmos. Sometimes, all you have to do is look up or reach down. I got lost somewhere along the way, but the Earth reminded me that I've always been home.

-

−Author Information−

If you have enjoyed these words and wish to find more by these wonderful authors, please explore their work on the following social media pages!

Sara Kelly
        Instagram @sara_kelly_poetry

Otthilia Poetria
        Instagram @otthilia_poetria

Barry Hollow
        Instagram @thehollowgram

L. T. Pelle
        Instagram @l.t.pelle

Adeline Gray
        Instagram @adelinewrites

Alan J.
        Instagram @alanj.chambers

Emily May Portillo
        Instagram @poetry.on.the.exhale

Emma Blas
        Instagram @emmablaspoetry

Lucia Haase
        Instagram @writer_in_residence

Jessica Walsh
        Instagram @her_odyssey

Wildflower
        Instagram @wildflower.musings

For more information regarding other A.B.Baird publications please visit us on our website on www.abbairdpublishing.com or on our Instagram page @a.b.baird_publishing

Symphonies of the Wild-Hearted

Dear Readers,

As always, we at A.B.Baird Publishing believe that all our writers are incredibly talented and encourage you to explore new writers often!

Your reviews mean more to us than you realize! One of the keys to continued success is having reviews on sites such as Amazon. If you have enjoyed this book we ask that you please let us know by leaving reviews on the amazon listing.

Our goals here at A.B.Baird Publishing center on continuing to empower writers by giving social media based authors as many avenues as possible towards publication. If you are interested in how you can become published, or want to stay up to date on our latest ventures, please join our email list on our website www.abbairdpublishing.com or visit us on Instagram @a.b.baird_publishing.

Thank you for your support- without you, we would be nothing!

Austie Baird – Owner
A.B.Baird Publishing

www.ingramcontent.com/pod-product-compliance
Lightning Source LLC
LaVergne TN
LVHW041248080426
835510LV00009B/646